Quantitative
Risk Assessment
For Environmental and
Occupational Health

Quantitative Risk Assessment For Environmental and Occupational Health

W. H. Hallenbeck and K. M. Cunningham

LEWIS PUBLISHERS, INC.

Library of Congress Cataloging-in-Publication Data

Hallenbeck, William H.
  Quantitative risk assessment for environmental and
occupational health.

  Bibliography: p.
  Includes index.
  1. Health risk assessment — Statistical methods.
  2. Environmental health — Statistical methods.
  3. Industrial hygiene — Statistical methods.
  I. Cunningham, K. M. (Kathleen M.)   II. Title.   [DNLM:
  1. Environmental Exposure.   2. Environmental Health.
  3. Environmental Pollutants — analysis.   4. Probability.
  WA 30 H184q]
  RA427.3.H35   1986   363.1   86-16117
  ISBN 0-87371-055-X

Library
University of Texas
at San Antonio

Third Printing 1988
Second Printing 1987

LEWIS PUBLISHERS, INC.
121 South Main Street, P.O. Drawer 519, Chelsea, Michigan 48118

PRINTED IN THE UNITED STATES OF AMERICA

To my Wife, Carolyn Hesse
To my Mother, Gladys Hallenbeck
To my Father, William Hallenbeck

To my Husband, Walter Cunningham
To my Daughter, Jessica Cunningham

PREFACE

Many individuals and groups need a usable treatment of the methodology required to assess the human health risks caused by toxicant exposure. This need is shared by industrial hygienists, environmental, occupational and public health professionals, toxicologists, epidemiologists, labor unions, attorneys, regulatory officials, and manufacturers and users of chemicals. The reader needs only a basic knowledge of biology and algebra in order to utilize the methodology presented. In addition, a basic knowledge of toxicology, epidemiology, and statistics is desirable for a full understanding of some aspects of risk assessment. Sophisticated computer programs are not required. All the computations can be carried out with a pocket calculator.

William H. Hallenbeck
Kathleen M. Cunningham

ACKNOWLEDGMENTS

The authors are grateful to Dr. Gil Zemansky, Chief Scientific/ Technical Section, Illinois Pollution Control Board, for identifying many important regulatory problems and pertinent literature.

The authors are indebted to Ms. Frederica Davis for the skill and dedication to detail she demonstrated during the preparation of the original manuscript.

William H. Hallenbeck holds a DrPH (Doctor of Public Health) degree in Environmental and Occupational Health Sciences from the University of Illinois at Chicago, a MSPH in Environmental Sciences and Engineering from the University of North Carolina at Chapel Hill, and a MS and BS in Chemistry from the State University of New York at Albany, New York.

Dr. Hallenbeck currently is an Associate Professor of Environmental and Occupational Health Sciences at the University of Illinois at Chicago (School of Public Health) where he teaches courses in risk assessment and radiological health.

Dr. Hallenbeck has conducted extensive laboratory and field research regarding the health effects of several environmental and occupational contaminants (asbestos, pesticides, ozone, sodium, fluoride, radon, radium, cadmium, acrylonitrile, styrene, and butadiene). Current research interests focus on risk assessment and management of environmental toxicants and methods for increasing the accuracy and precision of risk assessments. He has advised several private and governmental organizations in the area of health risk assessment.

Kathleen Cunningham received her BA degree in Biological Sciences and MA in Social Sciences with an emphasis on public policy for the University of Chicago. She received her PhD in Public Health from the University of Illinois at Chicago in the Environmental and Occupational Health Sciences Program.

Dr. Cunningham has conducted laboratory research in genetics and drug toxicity and has taught environmental health and ecology. Recent research activities have focused on chronic human health effects of pesticides, solvents and radioactive materials, primarily carcinogenic and reproductive effects. She is currently a research scientist at the New Jersey Department of Public Health in the environmental Health Protection Program.

CONTENTS

CHAPTER 1

Introduction

W. H. Hallenbeck

In recent years, the need to quantify the health risks associated with exposure to environmental and occupational toxicants has generated a new interdisciplinary methodology referred to as risk assessment. For given conditions of exposure, risk assessment (as defined in this volume) provides:

- a characterization of the types of health effects expected
- an estimate of the probability (risk) of occurrence of these health effects
- an estimate of the number of cases with these health effects
- a suggested acceptable concentration of a toxicant in air, water, or food

The outputs of risk assessment are necessary for informed regulatory decisions regarding worker exposures, plant emissions and effluents, ambient air and water exposures, chemical residues in foods, waste disposal sites, consumer products, and naturally occurring contaminants.

Risk assessment and risk management are an integral part of the contemporary regulatory activities of federal (FDA, 1979, 1985a, 1985b; OSHA, 1980, 1983, 1985; USEPA, 1980, 1984, 1985) and state agencies and the industries with which these agencies interact. This book is concerned only with risk assessment. Risk management refers to the selection and implementation of the most appropriate regulatory action based upon the results of risk assessment, available control technology, cost-benefit analysis, acceptable risk, acceptable number of cases, policy analysis, and social and political factors.

The major impetus for conducting risk assessments comes from federal legislation. Since 1972, federal health and safety statutes have adopted a general safety standard of "unreasonable risk" (e.g., Consumer Product Safety Act of 1972, the Federal Environmental Pesticide Control Act of 1972, and the Toxic Substances Control Act of 1976). These statutes do not contain a definition of the critical phrase "unreasonable risk" (Hutt, 1984). Recently several court decisions have helped to clarify the meaning of "unreasonable risk." U.S. courts recognize the legal doctrine referred to as *de minimus non curat lex*, or simply *de minimus*. This maxim holds that the law does not concern itself with trifling matters and that courts should be reluctant to apply the literal terms of a statute to mandate pointless results (FDA, 1985a). Courts have upheld this principle in their interpretations of the Food Additives Amendment, the Clean Air Act, the PCB provisions in the Toxic Substances Control Act, and the Occupational Safety and Health Act (FDA, 1985a; Hutt, 1984; OSHA, 1985). In its benzene decision, the U.S. Supreme Court indicated when a reasonable person might consider a risk significant (or unreasonable) and take steps to decrease it. The court stated:

> It is the Agency's [OSHA] responsibility to determine in the first instance what it considers to be a "significant" risk. Some risks are plainly acceptable and others are plainly unacceptable. If, for example, the odds are one in a billion that a person will die from cancer by taking a drink of chlorinated water, the risk clearly could not be considered significant. On the other hand, if the odds are one in a thousand that regular inhalation of gasoline vapors that are 2% benzene will be fatal a reasonable person might well consider the risk significant and take appropriate steps to decrease or eliminate it (OSHA, 1985).

Thus, OSHA is using an acceptable working lifetime risk of one in a thousand as a guide in determining permissible exposure levels for carcinogens (OSHA, 1985). In addition to the Supreme Court decision, OSHA is being guided in its determination of significant risk by the lifetime (45 years) work-related death rates for various occupations (OSHA, 1985):

- high-risk occupations (fire fighting and mining/quarrying): 27.45 per 1000 and 20.16 per 1000, respectively
- average-risk occupations (all manufacturing and all service employment): 2.7 per 1000 and 1.62 per 1000, respectively

- low-risk occupations (electrical equipment and retail clothing): 0.48 per 1000 and 0.07 per 1000, respectively

An acceptable risk of 10^{-3} is excessive. OSHA's overall *goal* should be to reduce the work-related death rates of all occupational sectors to that of the sector with the lowest work-related mortality, i.e., retail clothing at $0.07/1000 = 10^{-4}$. Also, it appears that OSHA is ignoring the additive effects caused by exposure to multiple carcinogens. (Synergistic effects are mentioned in Chapter 4.) For example, if a worker is exposed to 10 carcinogens each of which conveys a risk of 10^{-3}, the additive risk is 10^{-2}. Hence, it is recommended that OSHA use an acceptable risk of 10^{-5} or less as its goal. Of course, the attainment of this goal is subject to technological feasibility.

The FDA has interpreted several recent court decisions (excluding the benzene decision) to mean that a lifetime risk of one in a million is a *de minimus* level of cancer risk (i.e., insignificant and therefore acceptable) and is of no public health consequence (FDA, 1985a, 1985b). This level of risk translates into three excess cases per year ($10^{-6} \cdot 227 \cdot 10^6/74$) in a population of 227 million people with a life expectancy of 74 years. The USEPA also uses an acceptable risk of one in a million (USEPA, 1985). It appears that the FDA and USEPA would permit a lifetime risk of 10^{-6} for each contaminant. For example, if the general population has lifetime exposure to 100 carcinogenic chemicals, each of which conveys a lifetime acceptable risk of 10^{-6}, the additive lifetime risk is 10^{-4}, not 10^{-6}. Thus, an acceptable lifetime risk of 10^{-6} may not actually be as conservative as intended.

The Nuclear Regulatory Commission (NRC) has proposed higher acceptable lifetime risks than any other federal agency. NRC's acceptable lifetime risks (due to cancer mortality and serious hereditary effects) are $4 \cdot 10^{-2}$ for occupational exposure and $5 \cdot 10^{-3}$ for general population exposure (NRC, 1986).

Acceptable risks for the general population are frequently compared to the relatively higher lifetime risks of death which exist for many activities in the U.S. (Crouch and Wilson, 1984):

- selected occupational risks range from 0.004 (manufacturing) to 0.04 (mining and quarrying)
- selected accident risks range from 10^{-5} (bite/sting) to 0.02 (motor vehicle) and 0.04 (all types of accidents combined)
- selected sports risks range from 10^{-4} (ski racing) to 0.04 (parachuting) and 0.2 (professional stunting)

It must be remembered that there is a large component of individual discretion involved in the selection of one's occupation, sports activities, and living environment (the latter largely controls the probability of non-work related accidents). The presence of a toxicant in community air, water, or food usually constitutes an involuntary risk. It is important to distinguish between voluntary and involuntary risks. Most people would consider that these are two entirely separate classes of risk. People usually assume they are breathing risk-free air, drinking risk-free water, and eating risk-free food. Thus, the level of risk associated with breathing air, drinking water, and eating food is expected by most people to be far less than the risks involved in, for example, a career in mining, or professional stunting, or a sport like parachuting.

Another impetus for conducting risk assessments resulted from President Reagan's Executive Order 12291 (issued February 19, 1981). This order requires that certain agencies cannot undertake regulatory action unless:

- A need for regulation is adequately demonstrated.
- The potential benefits outweigh the potential costs and adverse effects.
- The most cost-effective and least burdensome approach is established (Zentner, 1984).

Thus, it can be appreciated that many individuals and groups need a usable treatment of the methodology required to assess the human health risks caused by toxicant exposure. This need is shared by industrial hygienists, environmental, occupational and public health professionals, toxicologists, epidemiologists, labor unions, attorneys, regulatory officials, and manufacturers and users of chemicals. Most interested parties do not have the expertise to evaluate risk(s) due to toxicant exposure. Furthermore, many of the published treatments of risk assessment are confusing due to impenetrable mathematics. This leaves interested parties suspicious of each other and with no recourse except to let the "experts" arrive at some acceptable level of exposure for the general population and/or workers. There is no justification for basing public policy on obscure methodology.

This book is designed to be readable and useful to those who need to assess the human health consequences of toxicant exposure. It will be especially valuable to those involved in the process of establishing acceptable concentrations of contaminants in air, water, and food. In order to reduce controversy and broaden the utilization of this work, every effort has been made to blend the overriding need to protect public and worker health with the need to use consensus-oriented methodologies.

A basic knowledge of biology and algebra is needed in order to utilize the methodology presented. In addition, a basic knowledge of toxicology, epidemiology, and statistics is desirable for a full understanding of some aspects of risk assessment. Sophisticated computer programs are not required. All the computations can be carried out with a pocket calculator.

1.1 CONTENTS

The chapters of this book are ordered in the same sequence of steps as one would use in performing an actual risk assessment: characterization of the exposure of a risk group, evaluation of experimental studies, calculation of risks and cases, and calculation of an acceptable concentration. "Risk group" refers to the actual or hypothetical exposed group for whom the risk assessment is being conducted. This group is composed of members of the general population and/or workers. "Experimental studies" refers to experimental animal or human epidemiology studies used to assess the significance of the risk group exposure.

Exposure characterization (Chapter 2) involves the definition of the chemical and physical properties of the toxicant, the routes of exposure, the environmental fate, the conditions of exposure (concentration and duration), and the nature of the risk group (age distribution, sex, size, and location). It is especially important to determine the exposure conditions of the risk group so that the most pertinent experimental studies can be selected for risk assessment. One of the primary goals of risk assessment is to match risk group and experimental group dose ranges in order to obviate the need to extrapolate beyond the experimental dose range. The health effects associated with exposure of any duration, up to and including lifetime, can be assessed.

The qualitative and quantitative evaluation of human and animal studies (Chapters 3 and 4) involves the weighing of many aspects of experimental studies. Many important concepts are presented in Chapter 3. Among the most important is the distinction between classes of toxicants which are known or assumed to have a threshold of response (sometimes referred to as nonzero threshold toxicants) and classes of toxicants which are known or assumed to have no threshold of response (sometimes referred to as zero threshold toxicants). A threshold toxicant is known or assumed to have no adverse effects below a certain dose; a nonthreshold toxicant is known or assumed to incur some risk of adverse response at all doses above zero.

Chapter 5 contains the methodology for calculating risks and cases for nonthreshold and threshold toxicants. The reader is shown how to utilize the data obtained via the criteria in Chapters 3 through 4.

The methods for determining the acceptable concentration of a toxicant in air, water, or food are presented in Chapter 6. These methods differ, depending on whether the health effect in question is known or assumed to have a threshold or nonthreshold dose-response relationship.

Finally, there are two chapters containing example risk assessments. Chapter 7 addresses community and worker exposure to a hypothetical industrial toxicant. This example closely follows the methodology presented in Chapters 2 through 6. Chapter 8 contains a detailed example of a risk assessment of a naturally occurring toxicant, radon. This example utilizes actual exposure and epidemiological data.

1.2 METHODS

Any equation can be used to fit experimental dose-response data. The only requirement is that the equation be a good predictor of response over the range of experimental doses. When a risk group is exposed to a dose that is within the experimental dose range, the estimate of risk can be calculated from the same equation used to fit the experimental dose-response data (Chapter 8). Experimental dose-response data can be used to predict both excess risk and number of excess cases for threshold and nonthreshold toxicants *when* the risk group dose is within the experimental dose range.

By definition, a threshold toxicant is presumed to convey no risk below the experimentally determined threshold dose. In this book, threshold toxicants are evaluated by determining the threshold dose, defining the values of several safety factors, and calculating an acceptable concentration.

Nonthreshold toxicants are evaluated differently because they are assumed to convey some risk at all doses above zero. The true shape of the dose-response relationship below the experimental dose range cannot be determined from experimental data, since an extremely large number of subjects would be required to detect small responses at very low doses. Even if such a massive experiment were conducted, it would yield an equation for only one chemical (Staffa and Mehlman, 1979). Hence, the form of the dose-response relationship in the subexperimental dose range must be assumed. Three classes of mathematical extrapolation models have been proposed for relating dose and response in the subexperimental dose range: tolerance distribution models (probit, logit, and Weibull), mechanistic models (one-hit, multihit, and multistage), and time-to-occurrence models (lognormal and Weibull). Also, individual models have been used: linear, quadratic, and linear-quadratic. Discussions of these models can be found in the following references: Altshuler, 1981; BEIR, 1980; Carlborg, 1981a, 1981b; FDA, 1985b (see Appendix 4); Gaylor et al., 1979, 1980; Hoel et al., 1975, 1980; Hogan, 1983; IRLG, 1979; Mantel and Bryan, 1961; Munro and Krewski, 1981; Van Ryzin, 1980.

In general, it is impossible to choose among these models based on their fit to experimental dose-response data, since they all usually fit with equal goodness. However, extrapolation below the experimental dose range usually results in divergences of predicted response of several orders of magnitude among the models (Krewski and Van Ryzin 1981). The linear and one-hit models yield about the same result in the very low dose range and usually are the most conservative in that they yield the highest risk per unit of dose and the lowest acceptable concentration.

When a model must be assumed for calculations in the subexperimental dose range, the linear model is recommended due to its conservatism, simplicity, and reliance on the single experimental dose-response data point which has the most ability to predict risk in the subexperimental dose range. The linear model consists of linear interpolation between the response observed at the lowest experimental dose and the origin at zero dose and zero response. Although the exact mechanism of toxicity can never be known with certainty in the subexperimental dose range, the mechanism operating at the lowest experimental dose is the one most likely to be the same as that mechanism which operates in the subexperimental dose range.

The overall goal of risk analysis in the subexperimental dose range is *to not underestimate* human risk. Since the linear model usually yields the highest risk per unit of dose in the very low-dose range, it is *unlikely* to underestimate risk. Also, the linear model utilizes the lowest significant experimental dose-response point; this feature reduces the risk of incorporating ineffective dose (see Section 3.2) in the analysis. Linear interpolation will be used throughout this book (Chapters 5–8).

1.3 LIMITATIONS

Risk assessments constitute a significant input to the decisionmaking process. It is very important that all sources of uncertainty and error accompany a risk assessment so that the limitations on the quantitative results are clearly understood. Uncertainty and error result from:

- poor definition of the experimental and/or risk group exposure, i.e., concentration, duration, chemical species, pertinent routes, dose rate
- use of experimental studies involving less-than-lifetime exposure or short observation periods
- use of experimental studies involving an inappropriate route of exposure
- toxicant interaction in the experimental studies or the risk group exposure
- failure to diagnose or misdiagnosis of the cause of morbidity or mortality
- misclassification of the exposure of individuals in a risk group due to complex daily patterns of movement
- pharmacokinetic and metabolic differences between species
- improper control groups
- extrapolation of experimental results into the very low-dose range
- differences between the experimental and risk groups regarding: age at first exposure, sex, confounding exposures, smoking habits, etc.

Most risk assessments contain one or more of these sources of uncertainty or error. In some cases, there will be sufficient knowledge to predict only the qualitative effects of uncertainty or error, e.g., under- or overprediction of risk. In other cases, the impact of sources of uncertainty or error can be presented in a quantitative sensitivity analysis. Risk assessment is in the early stages of development. There is much room for improvement via elimination of sources of uncertainty and error.

CHAPTER 2

Exposure Characterization

K. M. Cunningham

Risk estimates are developed based upon the exposure of the risk group. This chapter is designed to enable the reader to specify the following for a toxic exposure: who will be exposed, the concentration of exposure, the route of exposure, the duration of exposure, and the nature of exposure to any other toxic materials which are generated as a result of the release of a toxicant. This chapter provides guidelines and methodology for the evaluation and characterization of toxic exposures. The exposure information obtained through the methods given in this chapter is used in Chapter 3 to aid in the selection of appropriate animal or epidemiological studies for use in risk assessment.

The methods used to characterize exposure vary considerably depending on the circumstances surrounding exposure, i.e., the exposure scenario. Different models are used for air, surface water, groundwater and foodborne dispersion and contamination. This chapter does not provide specific guidelines for determining relevant exposure characteristics due to the widely varying nature and number of models available. Rather, it provides a general protocol for obtaining and evaluating information on concentration, duration, and routes of exposure and characterizing the risk group.

The accuracy with which exposure is characterized is a primary determinant of the ultimate validity of a risk assessment. Consequently, the risk assessor is urged to use environmental measurement data and actual population counts rather than estimates of these parameters whenever possible. To ensure adequate protection of the public's health, it is important to utilize upper estimates of exposure and population size.

Frequently, members of a risk group may be exposed via different contaminated media and routes. The Interagency Regulatory Liaison Group recommended consideration of each source of exposure independently (e.g., water, foods, air) to obtain the most complete description of exposure (IRLG, 1979). Other features of exposure which should be specified include whether the exposure is intentional or unintentional (e.g., pesticide residues in food vs nuclear power plant accidents) and voluntary or involuntary (e.g., elective X-rays vs passive smoking).

In some cases all the necessary information on exposure may already be available, and the reader could proceed directly to the evaluation of experimental studies discussed in Chapters 3 and 4. A list of required exposure information is given in Table 2.1. Usually all the information is not readily available, and it will be necessary to undertake considerable research in order to obtain a complete description of the exposure scenario, the toxicant, and the exposed group (risk group). For additional guidance on exposure characterization, the reader may wish to refer to USEPA guidelines for exposure assessment (USEPA, 1984).

Table 2.1. Exposure Characteristics

Trade names, common names, synonyms of toxicant
Chemical name and formula
Other materials formed during or following release
Fire or explosion hazards at all locations
Physical form of the material at all locations
Concentrations of material at all locations over the duration of the material's
    presence in any medium, e.g., air, water, food
Population distribution at all locations where exposure occurs (include number, age,
    and sex of all individuals)
Concentration and duration of exposure of all individuals (via any medium)

2.1 EXPOSURE SCENARIO

The circumstances surrounding exposure to a toxicant must be fully defined to obtain the exposure characteristics listed in Table 2.1. A description of the exposure scenario includes information on the source of the toxicant, the amount released and its chemical and physical form, a complete description of the area surrounding the release, and whether the material will be contained or distributed to a larger area.

The exposure scenario may be well defined if the exposure has already occurred. A hypothetical scenario may be described if the risk assessment is being undertaken to evaluate potential risks due to exposures which have not yet occurred. An exposure may be occurring, or have occurred, but not be well defined. If a complete description of the exposure scenario is not available, the risk assessor must obtain a description or develop a hypothetical description using the technical information which exists. It is important to note throughout the risk assessment which information is based upon estimates and which is based on real data (e.g., modeled air concentrations vs actual measurements). If estimates are used, their degree of uncertainty should be noted. If measurements are used, their potential error should be noted.

Usually a risk assessment will focus on a particular aspect of a toxicant's production, use, storage, or disposal. When the exposure scenario is very broadly defined, it becomes more difficult to assess the risks and there is greater uncertainty associated with the risk estimates. For example, in the siting of nuclear power plants, every aspect of the development, construction, operation, shutdown, and waste disposal is analyzed for health risks. Due to the number of people, functions, and materials involved, it is difficult to accurately predict actions and consequences which may result in toxic exposures.

Although there are various ways to proceed to obtain the necessary exposure information, one method is suggested here which may be generally applied. This should be modified, depending on the extent to which the risk assessor already has the necessary information.

A *preliminary* description of the exposure scenario should be obtained which answers the following questions:

- Where, when and how will the release of the toxicant occur?
- What is in the immediate vicinity of the release?
- What is the quantity, physical state and chemical identity of the released material?

Once the preliminary information is obtained, it *may* be necessary to refer to the characteristics of the toxicant discussed in Section 2.2 to further characterize the exposure. For example, if measurement data are not available, it is necessary to estimate concentrations using models. These models require information on material characteristics discussed in Section 2.2.

When the preliminary information listed above has been obtained regarding the exposure scenario, the following questions should be answered:

- What are the concentrations and durations of exposure in the area of the toxicant's release?
- Will the toxicant be distributed to a larger area, and if so what will be its form (physical and chemical), concentration, and duration of residence throughout the area of distribution? This description should include the concentrations at various locations and times throughout its residence, and it should include air- and waterborne materials as well as those taken up by biological materials such as plants and animals.

If it is not possible to answer the above questions using available data, it may be necessary to review the physical, chemical, and ecological characteristics of the toxicant discussed in Section 2.2 to determine the magnitude and nature of the exposure. Basic chemical and physical characteristics of the material which may be relevant to its toxicity include chemical composition, melting point, boiling point, density, molecular weight, and its mixture and reactivity with other materials present in the exposure environment.

The above characteristics indicate such critical features of exposure as whether the toxicant will be a liquid, solid, or gas during exposure. They also provide information necessary to determine the material's distribution, uptake, residence time, magnification and breakdown to new chemical compounds. Chemical and physical characteristics can also affect the intake, distribution, half-life, metabolism, and excretion of the toxicant by the risk group. For example, the compounding of a heavy metal with organic or inorganic chemicals may significantly alter its human toxicity.

If an exposure scenario is very complex or there are numerous potential exposure scenarios, it may be useful to set up an event-tree to clarify potential outcomes. Probabilities may be assigned to the various events to determine which outcomes are most likely. This can be used to establish priorities for conducting the risk assessment.

An event-tree is a diagrammatic representation of events which can occur. An example is given in Table 2.2 for the scenario of a toxic material container leak within a plant. By using such a diagram, the risk assessor is able to identify and organize the various exposure contingencies. For example, the event-tree in Table 2.2 shows that three different outcomes are possible: no contamination, plant contamination, or plant and ambient air contamination. Risk assessments could be done for the last two possibilities. However, if the likelihood that the three containment events (exterior vessel containment, ventilation system shutdown, cleanup) would all fail to occur is very small (e.g., 10^{-6}), it might be desirable to do a risk assessment only for a plant contamination scenario.

The assignment of various probabilities to events within a scenario has

Table 2.2. Event-Tree for Toxic Material Container Leak

Initiating Event: Crack in Material Container	Exterior Vessel Containment	Ventilation System Shutdown	Cleanup	
			FAILURE	Plant and ambient air contamination
		FAILURE	SUCCESS	Plant contamination only
	FAILURE	SUCCESS		No contamination
OCCURS				
DOES NOT OCCUR	SUCCESS			No contamination

been used extensively for evaluation of nuclear power plant risks. A discussion and critique of the methodology for that application is contained in *Probabilistic Risk Assessment* (GAO, 1985).

2.2   MATERIAL CHARACTERISTICS

A list of toxic material characteristics is given in Table 2.3. A review of the preliminary exposure scenario should be useful in determining which of the toxicant characteristics listed in Table 2.3 are relevant. For example, if the exposure scenario is the daily use of a toxicant in isolation from reactive materials at room temperature, it may not be relevant to obtain information on many of the physical, chemical, and biological characteristics, e.g., soil mobility. If indoor exposure were the only circumstance of concern to the risk group, data on ecological distribution would be irrelevant. However, if the scenario is an accidental release of a toxicant into the environment, with the potential for contact with numerous other reactive materials, it may be necessary to obtain all the information listed in Table 2.3.

Much information can be obtained from data systems accessible through large libraries, including the Chemical Information System (CIS), the Medical Literature Analysis and Retrieval System (MEDLARS), ORBIT, and DIALOG. The Hazardlines database provides a summary of most physical, chemical, biological, and toxicological data.

Based upon the data obtained for Table 2.3, the exposure scenario may need to be expanded. It may also indicate the limits of exposure. For example, if a toxicant is reactive with air or water, the exposure scenario may include explosion or fire rather than a simple release of the substance into the immediate environment. If a toxicant rapidly degrades to a nontoxic material following release into the air, the exposure scenario might be geographically limited to a much smaller area than would be the case for a toxicant with greater stability.

If more than one toxicant is present or formed due to a toxicant's release, data should be obtained for each material. Information on the interactive effects of multiple toxicants may also be important. Of course, this is imperative if the materials are chemically reactive. It may also be important if they are biologically active; they may have antagonistic, synergistic, or totally independent toxic effects in the human body, or one may alter the action of another in the environment.

Characterization of toxicants should include *all* materials which are potential human hazards, *even if they are not listed as the active or toxic*

Table 2.3.   Toxic Material Characteristics

Trade names, common names, synonyms

Physical characteristics
    molecular weight
    melting point
    boiling point
    density
    vapor pressure

Chemical characteristics
    chemical composition
    solubility
    stability (include fire and explosion hazard)
    impurities
    compounding or carrier (if applicable)
    pH
    reactivity with other materials including containers:

material	*reactivity*	*compounds formed*[a]	*hazard*[b]

Ecological characteristics
    foliar degradation/plant metabolism
    aqueous degradation
    soil, air, and water degradation
    animal metabolism
    bioaccumulation potential
    soil mobility
    systemic plant uptake from soil
    significant terminal residues
    environmental fate

[a]The characteristics, exposure, and risks associated with each compound formed during a potential reaction with the toxic material must be evaluated separately.
[b]Hazards due to the reaction itself.

ingredient. Solvents and other ingredients which may not be the principal or active ingredients in a mixture are frequently toxic. For example, carbon tetrachloride, gasoline, and benzene have been used as solvents and "inert" ingredients.

Once the preliminary questions regarding the toxicant's release have been answered, and the physical and chemical characteristics are known, various models can be used to calculate contaminant concentrations in air and water following a release. There are numerous air dispersion models available. A selection of models which have been developed for the USEPA's Office of Air Quality Planning and Standards is available through the National Technical Information Service. Many of these are variations of a Gaussian plume model. An excellent resource for information on groundwater models is the International Groundwater Modeling Center in Indianapolis, Indiana. Surface water models have been developed by Battelle Northwest Laboratories, Oak Ridge National Laboratory and other groups. SERATRA is a frequently recommended surface water model.

Depending upon the exposure scenario, the ecological distribution of a toxic material may be of concern. To obtain information on the ecological characteristics (see Table 2.3), the risk assessor is referred to data which chemical manufacturers and federal and state agencies have on file for many chemicals. Testing has been required for many materials, such as pesticides, and the results of the research can be obtained from the USEPA.

Unless risk assessors are familiar with air, water, or ecological modeling, it is recommended that specialists in these areas be consulted for assistance. In the ideal case, the risk assessor will be provided with information regarding the concentrations and durations of exposure at all relevant locations, thus obviating the need to undertake the modeling calculations. Whether actual measurements or estimates based on models are obtained, upper bound concentrations should be used in risk assessments.

2.3   RISK GROUP CHARACTERISTICS

The location, exposure concentrations, and exposure durations must be specified for each member of a risk group. All individuals exposed at levels above background comprise the risk group. For many toxicants which are not commonly found in the environment, there is no background level. Consequently, all individuals exposed at detectable levels would be considered at risk.

It is usually necessary to obtain information on both population location and behavior to adequately characterize exposure. For example, people who travel to work or other activities away from their homes may spend only a portion of the day in a contaminated residential area. Other people might travel into the contaminated area for various activities. If exposure were via food products, dietary habits would be of concern. A review of the behavior of subgroups of those exposed may reveal individuals with especially high exposures who incur higher risks.

Many toxicants have effects which may differ based upon the age or sex of the exposed individuals. Consequently, these population characteristics may be needed to conduct the risk assessment. The risk assessor may wish to evaluate health effects studies as discussed in Chapters 3 and 4 before obtaining more detailed population data to determine if information on age, sex or other population characteristics is relevant. For example, in some cases a hypersusceptible subgroup of the population, e.g., asthmatics, may be identified as having unique risk characteristics through a review of health effects studies.

When the exposure scenario, toxic material characteristics, and the risk group have been fully characterized, the risk assessor should be able to specify all the exposure characteristics listed in Table 2.1.

An example of an exposure scenario and the type of data required for the risk assessment is given below.

A rail accident results in the release of compound X into the immediate environment. The compound is non-volatile and reaches a river in the vicinity which is used as a drinking water supply for the population which lives along the river. Due to runoff and other dilution water which enters the river, the toxicant is diluted to an undetectable level 50 miles from the release. The toxic material is hydrolyzed to a non-toxic form approximately 48 hours after release into the river.

The data below were obtained using a surface water contaminant dispersion model to estimate the concentration of toxic material at various locations along the river. The population drinking the water at each location was determined and the exposure concentration and duration were calculated.

Location Along River	Population Size	Average 48-hr Concentration	Duration
(mi)		(mg/l)	(hr)
0–5	105	20	48
5–25	250	15	48
25–40	370	10	48
40–50	240	5	48

Route: ingestion only.

2.4 SUMMARY

A complete characterization of exposure to a toxic substance will enable the risk assessor to specify the exposure concentration, duration, and route for the risk group. The following table can be used to summarize the relevant information on exposure. The physical and chemical information discussed in Section 2.2 may be relevant to the evaluation of health effects discussed in Chapters 3 and 4, but it is not listed in Table 2.4 since the quantity of this type of data may range from a few lines to a few pages.

Table 2.4. Summary of Population Exposure Data

Number Exposed (specify age and sex)	Concentration	Duration	Route (dermal, oral, inhalation)

CHAPTER 3

Qualitative Evaluation of Human
and Animal Studies

W. H. Hallenbeck and K. M. Cunningham

This chapter contains detailed discussions of the various qualitative characteristics of human and animal studies which must be evaluated prior to the selection and application of appropriate studies in a risk assessment. Some criteria for study selection are specific to the requirements of risk assessment. For example, it is essential that a study used in a risk assessment have clearly quantified dose and response data. Although epidemiological studies can indicate causality, they are not useful in a risk assessment when exposure is not quantified. Information and guidance which are useful in the qualitative evaluation of human and animal studies have been organized into the following sections:

- Control data
- Latent period, effective exposure, and followup
- Matching of experimental and risk groups
- Animal studies: special considerations
- Epidemiology studies: special considerations
- Classification of toxicants by health effect and dose-response character
- Data bases

3.1 CONTROL DATA

The type of control group used in an epidemiology study is a major determinant of whether or not statistically significant adverse effects can be detected in a test (exposed) group. In most epidemiology studies, the test group is composed of workers who are exposed to one or more chemicals. For maximum study sensitivity, the control group should be drawn from workers in the same or a similar industrial setting who are exposed to lower or zero levels of the chemical under study.

The general U.S. population is frequently used as a control group. It is not the ideal control group because it includes a higher proportion of ill people. Death rates for the general population are twice those for an age- and sex-matched worker group (Najarian, 1978). This discrepancy between the health status of the general population and that of workers may lead to a "healthy worker effect" in epidemiology studies, i.e., the high rate of incidence in the general population could prevent the detection of statistically significant adverse effects in an exposed worker group. Hence, it is preferable to use an epidemiology study where the control group was drawn from another worker group matched for all covariates except exposure.

It is much easier to match test and control groups in an animal bioassay since, theoretically at least, all variables can be matched, e.g., species, strain, sex, age, diet. However, sometimes there is strong evidence that an uncontrolled effect has occurred in either the test or control group which could confound the results of the bioassay. There are three standard ways of checking data for uncontrolled effects in long-term studies: analyses of weight and survival data and use of historical controls.

A gross difference between the weight vs time curves of the test and control animals indicates that there was a major disruption of normal homeostasis in the test animals. The disruption was most likely due to high-level dosing. In the absence of unusual morbidity or premature mortality, large differences in weight gain may be the only indication that the test dose was too high. The larger the difference in weight gain, the more likely the results of the experiment are confounded by uncontrolled factors such as abnormal metabolism.

A gross difference between the survival vs time curves of test and control animals may indicate the presence of an uncontrolled effect. Premature deaths in the test or control groups may be caused by unusual events, such as contamination of a selected batch of animal feed, infectious disease in one of the groups, or a test dose which was too high.

If a comparison of survival curves indicates that there were premature deaths in the test group, the number at risk must be adjusted downward when the response under consideration is latent (e.g., cancer). For a latent response, an animal is considered at risk only if it survived from the time of first exposure for a period at least as long as the minimum latent period. Reducing the number at risk in the test group will usually increase the statistical significance of a positive finding. Of course, if there is no response observed in the test group, the validity of the study decreases as the number of premature deaths increases.

Excessive premature deaths in the control group may necessitate comparing the results in the test group to those observed in historical controls. Historical control data for a particular species and strain are derived from years of observation of hundreds or even thousands of control animals.

There are two types of control response which may be inaccurately characterized by a single control group of finite size. A rare response with a low background incidence may not even be observed in a finite control sample. Thus, a given test group may appear to have a significantly increased incidence when compared to that of a small control group. However, when the test response is compared to the historical control response, there may be no difference. The other type of control response is one which occurs with a broad range of incidences in finite control samples. Again, the test results should be compared to historical controls whenever the response in a finite control sample is known to be unstable.

3.2 LATENT PERIOD, EFFECTIVE EXPOSURE, AND FOLLOWUP

Many toxicants produce health effects immediately following exposure, and for those health effects there is no latent period. For example, liver damage resulting from exposure to a solvent or kidney damage following exposure to a heavy metal can usually be detected within hours or days following first exposure. Alternatively, some effects, most notably cancers, are not detectable until months or years following first exposure.

Latent period is the time between the initial induction of a health effect and the manifestation (or detection) of the health effect. Induction may occur after a single exposure, repeated exposure, or only after continuous exposure. The exposure which results in the induction of a latent effect is referred to as the effective exposure. In order to determine the effective exposure time and the latent period, it is necessary to know when induction occurred. If a study involves only one exposure, or exposure over a short period of time, the point in time of induction can be estimated. However, animal and epidemiological studies usually involve long-term exposures which preclude the precise determination of the point in time of induction. In this case, the latent period is crudely estimated as the minimum, median, or maximum time (or some fraction of the time) from first exposure to the detection of the latent effect.

There is also some imprecision associated with the detection of the health effect. Since detection can involve either microscopic identification of pathology or observation of gross pathology, the latent period will vary depending on the method used to evaluate the experimental subjects. For example, microscopic pathology could usually be detected prior to gross morphological changes.

In spite of the difficulty in determining the actual latent period associated with an exposure and effect, it is necessary to estimate the latent period to obtain an accurate estimate of risk. The median latent period is used to calculate effective dose (Chapters 4 and 5) and the minimum latent period is used to calculate excess cases per year (Chapter 5).

The latent period has an impact on the calculation of dose because the dose delivered during this period is likely to be ineffective. An example of this is the induction of lung cancer by the radioactive emissions of radon and radon daughters (Chapter 8). The minimum latent period of lung cancer due to radon exposure is estimated to be 15 years (Geddes, 1979; Edling and Axelson, 1983; Samet et al., 1984). Therefore, the 15 years prior to the detection of lung cancer are not relevant to the observation of lung cancer, and exposure which occurred during those 15 years should not be included in dose or exposure calculations.

The latent periods of cancers vary considerably among individuals and types of cancers. For example, although the minimum latent period for radon-induced lung cancer is approximately 15 years, the median latent period from first exposure may be more than 40 years (Radford and St. Clair Renard, 1984a). The distribution of latent periods for a specific toxicant and effect may be normal; however, not enough is known about latent periods to make generalizations for all types of exposures and cancers.

The risk assessor may need to obtain information in addition to that found in the animal or epidemiological studies in order to define the minimum and median latent periods. Human pathology and veterinary pathology texts do not provide information on latent periods for cancers resulting from exposures to specific materials. However, they do provide general guidelines on the latent periods of most cancers. If more specific information is not available, the general guidelines can be used with an understanding of their limitations.

A study must follow the subjects beyond the length of the minimum latent period to observe all effects associated with exposure. Under ideal circumstances a study will follow subjects for their lifetime. This provides for the observation of all effects due to exposure. While this is often done in chronic animal studies, it is not common in epidemiological studies. Epidemiological studies are limited in their followup of subjects by the extended lifetime of humans, which makes lifetime followup difficult and expensive. If a historical prospective epidemiological study (one which studies an exposure which occurred in the past and follows the exposed individuals forward in time to the present) is used, there may be an adequate followup period. However, quantifying exposure in the past and following subjects over decades is problematic, and these types of studies are not common. Epidemiological studies more often have a relatively short followup period which cannot capture all the cases attributable to exposure.

Either animal or epidemiological studies which do not have a followup period at least as long as the minimum latent period will result in an undercounting of cases and an underestimate of risk. When selecting studies for use in a risk assessment, the risk assessor should attempt to obtain studies with followup periods as long as the maximum latent period of the effect under consideration. If a positive epidemiology study is used which has a less than ideal followup period, it is incumbent on the risk assessor to highlight the fact that risk most likely has been underestimated. (Chapter 5 contains more discussion of this idea.)

If the followup period is shorter than the minimum latent period, the study may erroneously conclude that there was no effect. The risk assessor should review studies with a negative outcome for this study design deficit before concluding that no effects are associated with an exposure.

3.3 MATCHING OF EXPERIMENTAL AND RISK GROUPS

The risk assessor should select epidemiological or animal studies with characteristics which match the characteristics of the risk group as closely as possible. The characteristics of greatest concern to the risk assessor are: species, age at first exposure, sex, dose, dose rate, and pathology. (Dose is discussed in Chapters 4 and 5.)

The use of an epidemiological study is preferable to an animal study because the biological systems of epidemiological subjects are similar to those of the risk group with respect to uptake, distribution, deposition, activation, detoxification, retention, and excretion of the toxicant. These features can affect response, and may not be similar across species. The significant problems associated with dose conversions from animals to humans (Chapter 4) can be avoided by using epidemiological studies. In addition, questions related to the latent period and nature of the exposure-induced health effects are less ambiguous if epidemiological studies are used. If animal studies are selected, the species most similar to humans or the most sensitive species with respect to the toxicant and target organ should be used.

The age at which exposure occurs may be a critical factor contributing to the level of cancer risk. Studies have shown higher cancer risks associated with exposure to some toxicants in both children and the elderly (Upton, 1984; BEIR, 1980; Wakabayashi et al., 1983). Animal experiments have yielded mixed results regarding the importance of age at first exposure and cancer risk (BEIR, 1980). The relationship between age and risk may vary by both the type of toxicant and the nature of the health effect. Due to the impact which age may have on risk, studies should be selected to match the age of first exposure of the experimental subjects to those of the risk group.

Due to the numerous physiological differences between males and females, it is advisable to match experimental subjects to the risk group with respect to sex. Some health effects appear to be influenced by hormone levels (e.g., breast cancer) and many are sex specific (e.g., reproductive disorders). Consequently, a less accurate determination of the types of response and their incidence may be obtained if the experimental and risk groups are not well matched.

The risk assessor should match the cumulative dose (the total dose delivered) of the experimental group to that of the risk group to obtain the best risk estimate. As discussed in Chapter 1, the behavior of the dose-response curve cannot be predicted in the low-dose range. Consequently, the most accurate risk predictions result when risk group doses are within the range of animal or epidemiological studies. (Methods for determining the cumulative dose of the experimental and risk groups are presented in Chapters 4 and 5.) Dose rate (e.g., mg/kg body weight/day) has been shown to affect risk for some toxic materials. For example, some types of radiation generate higher risks at lower dose rates (Mays et al., 1978; BEIR, 1980; Upton, 1984; Chameaud et al., 1977). Different dose rates can also produce different health effects. For example, acute exposure to toluene may produce coma. However, chronic low-level toluene exposure causes renal damage and blood disorders (Hallenbeck and Cunningham-Burns, 1985).

Although the overriding concern in matching dose is to obtain correspondence between the cumulative doses of the experimental and risk groups, the dose rates should be matched whenever possible. When occupational studies are used to predict risk for a general population risk group, differences in dose rate must be noted since workers have an 8-hour exposure period per day.

Exposure to most toxicants can cause numerous health effects. A separate risk assessment must be conducted for each type of health effect unless the experimental data indicate identical dose-response behavior is occurring for each health effect. (The problems associated with multiple disease manifestations in the same experimental subjects are treated in Chapter 4.) The risk assessor should ascertain the specific type of pathology associated with a toxic exposure. It is suggested that the same International Classification of Diseases (ICD) codes be used for the epidemiological subjects and the risk group.

3.4 ANIMAL STUDIES: SPECIAL CONSIDERATIONS

Numerous factors in animal studies can be evaluated to aid in determining the validity of the study results. Those factors common to both animal and epidemiological studies are discussed elsewhere in Chapter 3, and in Chapter 4. This section deals with the unique features of animal studies which are of importance to the risk assessor. The reader should note that information on the features discussed in this section is not always included in the published reports of animal studies. However, if the study results are unusual or merit further investigation due to their importance, the risk assessor may wish to contact the authors of the animal study for more detail or clarification.

The selection of the appropriate species is critically important to obtaining an accurate risk estimate. Although no animal will provide a biological system identical to that of humans, some species have much greater similarity in their responses to specific toxicants. The risk assessor is urged to obtain this information from the literature, because species susceptibility and response vary by both target system and toxicant. Due to the thousands of toxicants which could be evaluated via risk assessment, a comprehensive review of species responsiveness is beyond the scope of this book. For the maximum protection of the public's health, the risk assessor should select the studies which utilize the most sensitive species (those with the greatest response per unit of dose) in the dose range of concern.

Guidance regarding selection of appropriate species may be obtained from the Institute of Laboratory Animal Resources (Institute of Laboratory Animal Resources, National Research Council, 2101 Constitution Avenue, N.W., Washington, D.C. 20418) or the American Association for Accreditation of Laboratory Animal Care (American Association for Accreditation of Laboratory Animal Care, 208A North Decar Road, New Lenox, Illinois 60451). The reader is also referred to the following:

Animals for Medical Research: Models for the Study of Human Disease. B. M. Mitruka, H. M. Rawnsley, and D. V. Vadehra. (New York: John Wiley & Sons, Inc., 1976).
Bibliography of Induced Animal Models of Human Disease. G. Hegreberg and C. Leathers, eds. (Pullman, WA: Washington State University, 1981).
Bibliography of Naturally Occurring Animal Models of Human Disease. G. Hegreberg and C. Leathers, eds. (Pullman, WA: Washington State University, 1981).
Spontaneous Animal Models of Human Disease. E. J. Andrews, B. C. Ward, and N. H. Altman, Eds. (New York: Academic Press, 1979).

The quality of an animal study and the accuracy of its results depend, in part, on the care which is taken in the study to ensure that the animal responses can be clearly identified and that dose is delivered appropriately and accurately. If the health of the experimental animals is impaired by factors other than intended toxicant exposure, the validity of the animal response data is jeopardized. If adequate care is not taken of the experimental animals, individuals may be lost to followup through premature death or the need to use therapies inconsistent with the experimental protocol to treat illnesses unrelated to the toxicant exposure. This can result in invalid results, including false negative results due to a diminished sample size. Disease and disturbances among experimental animals can also directly confound the experimental results by altering responses to toxicants.

The United States Department of Agriculture, the National Institutes of Health, and the Food and Drug Administration have established guidelines for animal care and experimentation in an attempt to provide quality control of the results. The reader is referred to the Guide for the Care and Use of Laboratory Animals and the Animal Welfare Act for detailed descriptions of proper experimental animal treatment (NIH, 1985; CFR, 1984). The guidelines specify needs with respect to: space, light levels and cycles, activity of the animals, temperature, humidity, ventilation, noise levels, dietary adequacy and contamination, bedding materials, water supply, sanitation, handling, and qualifications of caregivers and supervisory personnel.

These factors are known to affect animals' responses to toxicants. For example, elevated temperature and humidity can cause increased susceptibility of rodents to toxic agents (Baetjer, 1968). They can also induce pathological states. For example, high noise levels can lead to eosinopenia, elevated adrenal weights, and reduced fertility in rodents (Geber et al., 1966; Nayfield and Besch, 1981; Zondeck and Tamari, 1964), and increased blood pressure in primates (Peterson et al., 1981).

Responses to toxicant exposure can also be altered due to contaminants in the environment. Exposure to food contaminants or aromatic hydrocarbons from cedar and pine bedding materials can induce hepatic enzymes and thus alter responses to the numerous toxicants which interact with that enzyme system (Newberne, 1975; Vesell, 1967; Cunliffe-Beamer et al., 1981; NIH, 1985).

In addition to ensuring animal health, the study design must ensure that the dose of the toxicant can be appropriately measured. For example, if the toxicant is contained in food offered *ad lib*, the daily food intake should be weighed. When standard intake rates are relied upon to estimate dose, an erroneous dose may be reported because some toxicants and the pathological states they induce cause appetite reduction. Procedures must also be designed to minimize the possibility of contamination between test and control groups or two test groups (Sansone and Losikoff, 1979). The same animals should never be used to evaluate the effects of two or more toxicants simultaneously unless the goal of the study is to determine their combined effects. The chances for confounding of effects is too great.

In summary, the risk assessor may wish to evaluate the factors mentioned in this section in detail for those animal studies which are critically important to a risk assessment or those which indicate very unusual results and merit further consideration.

3.5 EPIDEMIOLOGICAL STUDIES: SPECIAL CONSIDERATIONS

Various factors are of importance to the evaluation of epidemiological studies which are unique or must be reviewed with special attention. Those discussed in this section include the following: exposure quantification, the use of epidemiological terminology, problems associated with retrospective and prospective studies, and confounding exposures.

Epidemiological studies were originally developed to investigate associations bewteen a health-related attribute (e.g., cholera, lung cancer, hemophilia) and a factor which contributed to that attribute (e.g., exposure to contaminated water, cigarettes, genetic defects). A classic example is a study of exposed and nonexposed groups with a comparison of the proportion in each group having a specific disease. Such a study *could* establish an association between exposure and the health effect without quantifying exposure. Many epidemiological studies are still carried out with little or no exposure quantification. Consequently, a large number of epidemiological studies cannot be used in risk assessment because risk assessment methodology requires well quantified exposures and responses.

Epidemiological studies often present a quantification of the degree of response among subjects. Various terms are used to express this idea. Although risk assessment methodology utilizes primarily incidence information, the risk assessor must be familiar with other epidemiological terms because it is sometimes necessary to back-calculate incidence from epidemiological data given in other terms (Chapter 4). Common terms and their meanings are given in Table 3.1. The terms incidence, SMR, and RR will be used in Chapter 4.

Two types of epidemiological studies are commonly reported: retrospective (case control) and prospective (cohort) studies. A retrospective study looks back in time at the exposure history of individuals who have the health effect (cases) and at a group who do not (controls). Retrospective studies are more common in cases when the health effect under consideration has a long latent period. These types of studies can be done relatively quickly and inexpensively and are encountered frequently.

Table 3.1. Epidemiological Terms

Term	Meaning
incidence rate	$\dfrac{\text{number of new cases over a period of time}}{\text{population at risk}}$
prevalence rate	$\dfrac{\text{number of existing cases at a point in time}}{\text{total population}}$
standard mortality ratio (SMR)	$\dfrac{\text{observed deaths}}{\text{expected deaths}}$
proportionate mortality ratio (PMR)	$\dfrac{\text{deaths from a specific cause and in a period of time}}{\text{total deaths in the same time period}} \times 100$
relative risk (RR) (synonym: risk ratio)	$\dfrac{\text{incidence among exposed}}{\text{incidence among nonexposed}}$
attributable risk (synonym: risk difference)	incidence among exposed − incidence among nonexposed

However, they rely on past events and are subject to errors in recording and memory. There is also a greater opportunity for bias among both the subjects and researchers in this type of study (Mausner and Bahn, 1974). A serious problem with retrospective studies is the selection of inappropriate controls. Controls are sometimes selected from a similar occupational group in the case of an occupational study or from patients in a hospital or clinic. If the basis for their selection (e.g., employment in a certain occupation or the treatment of a particular disease at the hospital or clinic) is related either positively or negatively to the exposure being investigated, the study results may be inaccurate (Jick and Miettinen, 1973). An example of this is discussed in Chapter 8. The appropriate selection of controls was discussed in more detail in Section 3.1.

Prospective studies follow a group of people, all of whom are initially free of the health effect under consideration and who have different levels of exposure to the toxicant in question. Due to the design of this type of study, a health effect with a long latent period will require a long-term study. This makes prospective studies difficult and expensive. It also makes them impractical for circumstances which require rapid results. For example, it is usually not possible to wait decades to determine if a suspected carcinogen causes cancer. An additional problem associated with prospective studies is that very large cohorts must be followed if the health effect in question has a low incidence. For example, to obtain 1833 lung cancer cases in studies of smoking and lung cancer, over one million people were followed (Mausner and Bahn, 1974). The risk assessor should note whether the sample size is adequate if negative results are obtained in a prospective study when other studies have shown positive results. For methods to calculate sample size refer to: *Statistical Methods for Rates and Proportions*, J. L. Fleiss, John Wiley & Sons, New York, 1973.

Due to the long latent period of some health effects, most notably cancers, it is often difficult to establish causality between exposure and response. The difficulty in following human populations over many decades, noting all relevant factors, and the numerous confounding exposures which can occur make epidemiological studies difficult, expensive, and prone to error.

The problem of confounding exposures can occur in animal or epidemiological studies, but it is much more likely to occur in epidemiological studies due to the inability of researchers to control many variables in human exposure and activities. A confounding exposure occurs when exposure to a toxicant other than the one under study causes an increase or decrease in response. For example, if a suspected respiratory carcinogen were being studied and there was a high proportion of smokers among the exposed group which was not noted by the researchers, the results might indicate a spurious or erroneously strong association between lung cancer and the suspected carcinogen. Since most environments contain some contaminants (e.g., formaldehyde, radon, carbon monoxide), an epidemiological study should indicate whether confounding contaminants were considered, especially in occupational studies. The problem of confounding exposures is sometimes dealt with through the careful selection of controls with very similar environments. Controls were discussed in Section 3.1.

Other factors which should be considered by risk assessors because they often lead to erroneous results in epidemiological studies include the following:

- the use of nonrandom samples of the risk group
- nonparticipation of a segment of the risk group
- variation in making and recording observations of response by the medical and study personnel
- variations in perceptions of health effects and health-related behavior by subjects
- variations in the availability of health care resources

Although numerous potential sources of error exist in epidemiological studies, a well designed epidemiological study is preferable to an animal study due to the advantages of observing the dose-response results in a human rather than an animal population.

3.6 CLASSIFICATION OF TOXICANTS BY HEALTH EFFECT AND DOSE-RESPONSE CHARACTER

The spectrum of health effects caused by chemicals can be arbitrarily divided into four classes: cancer (which includes somatic mutations), germ-cell mutations, developmental effects, and organ/tissue effects (e.g. reproductive organ damage and neurological damage). Each class of health effects poses unique regulatory problems largely due to problems associated with extrapolating experimental results to humans. One of the most important problems in extrapolation is defining the character of the dose-response relationship for a class of health effects.

Current regulatory practice is to classify chemicals as having a zero threshold (sometimes referred to as nonthreshold) or nonzero threshold (sometimes referred to as threshold) dose-response relationship. The consensus of current scientific opinion is that:

- All carcinogens should be assumed to be genotoxic and have zero threshold dose-response relationship.
- Mutagens have a zero threshold dose-response relationship.
- Developmental toxicants have a nonzero threshold dose-response relationship.
- Organ/tissue toxicants have a nonzero threshold dose-response relationship.

Acceptable concentrations for nonzero threshold chemicals are computed using the safety factor method, whereas acceptable concentrations for zero threshold chemicals are established via the risk analysis method. These two methods of establishing acceptable concentrations are discussed in Chapter 6.

Sometimes a chemical will produce multiple types of health effects. Whenever both dose-response models apply to a single chemical, the lowest acceptable concentration (calculated from either method) is recommended for adoption.

3.6.1. Carcinogens

Chemical carcinogenesis refers to the induction of neoplasms that are not usually observed, the earlier induction of neoplasms that are commonly observed, and/or the induction of more neoplasms than are usually found. Etymologically, carcinogenesis means the induction of malignant neoplasms. However, the commonly accepted meaning is the induction of malignant or benign tumors. The terms tumor and neoplasm are used synonomously. Tumorigen, oncogen, and blastomogen are used synonomously with carcinogen, although occasionally tumorigen may refer to a chemical that induces only benign tumors (IARC, 1984).

The USEPA has published proposed guidelines for the classification of the weight of evidence for human carcinogenicity (USEPA, 1984). These guidelines are adapted from those of the International Agency for Research on Cancer (IARC, 1984) and consist of the categorization of the weight of evidence into five groups (Groups A-E): human carcinogens, probable human carcinogens, possible human carcinogens, not classified, and no evidence of carcinogenicity for humans.

Group A—Human Carcinogens

There is sufficient evidence from epidemiologic studies to support a causal association between exposure to the agent and cancer. Three criteria must be met before a causal association can be inferred between exposure and cancer in humans: (1) there is no identified bias which could explain the association, (2) the possibility of confounding has been considered and ruled out as explaining the association, and (3) the association is unlikely to be due to chance. In general, although a single study may be indicative of a cause-effect relationship, confidence in inferring a causal association is increased when several independent studies are concordant in showing the association, when the association is strong, when there is a dose-response relationship, or when a reduction in exposure is followed by a reduction in the incidence of cancer.

Group B—Probable Human Carcinogens

This category includes agents for which the evidence of human carcinogenicity from epidemiologic studies ranges from almost sufficient to inadequate. To reflect this range, the category is divided into higher (Group B1) and lower (Group B2) degrees of evidence. Usually, category B1 is reserved for agents for which there is at least limited evidence of carcinogenicity to humans from epidemiologic studies. Limited evidence of carcinogenicity indicates that a causal interpretation is credible but that alternative explanations such as chance, bias, or confounding could not be excluded. Inadequate evidence indicates that one of two conditions prevailed: (a) there were few pertinent data, or (b) the available studies, while showing evidence of association, did not exclude chance, bias, or confounding.

When there are inadequate data for humans, it is reasonable to regard agents for which there is sufficient evidence of carcinogenicity in animals as if they presented a carcinogenic risk to humans. Therefore, agents for which there is inadequate evidence from human studies and sufficient evidence from animal studies would usually result in a classification of B2. Sufficient evidence of carcinogenicity indicates that there is an increased incidence of malignant tumors or combined malignant and benign tumors: (a) in multiple species or strains, or (b) in multiple experiments, or (c) to an unusual degree with regard to incidence, site or type of tumor, or age at onset. Additional evidence may be provided by data on dose-response effects, as well as information from short-term tests or on chemical structure. In some cases, the known chemical or physical properties of an agent and the results from short-term tests allow its transfer from B2 to B1.

Regarding the use of short-term mutagenesis data, the following cautions must be observed due to the limitations of current knowledge about mechanisms of carcinogenesis (IARC, 1984):

- At present, short-term tests alone should not be used to conclude whether or not an agent is carcinogenic, nor can they predict reliably the relative potencies of compounds as carcinogens in intact animals.
- The currently available tests do not detect all classes of agents that are active in the carcinogenic process (e.g., hormones).
- Negative results from short-term tests cannot be considered as evidence to rule out carcinogenicity, nor does lack of demonstrable genetic activity attribute an epigenetic (i.e., nongenetic) or any other property to a substance.

Regarding the use of chemical structure, there is a limited base of empirical data that correlates carcinogenic potential and molecular structure. Presently, the consensus of the scientific community is that molecular structure has limited value in identifying carcinogens and mutagens and is to be used only as correlative supporting evidence (IRLG, 1979).

Group C—Possible Human Carcinogens

There is limited evidence of carcinogenicity in animals in the absence of human data. Limited evidence means that the data suggest a carcinogenic effect, but are limited because: (a) the studies involve a single species, strain, or experiment, or (b) the experiments are restricted by inadequate dosage levels, inadequate duration of exposure to the agent, inadequate period of followup, poor survival, too few animals, or inadequate reporting, or (c) an increase in the incidence of benign tumors only.

Group C includes a wide variety of evidence: (a) definitive malignant tumor response in a single well conducted experiment, (b) marginal tumor response in studies having inadequate design or reporting, (c) benign but not malignant tumors, with an agent showing no response in a variety of short-term tests for mutagenicity, and (d) marginal responses in a tissue known to have a high and variable background rate.

In some cases, the known physical or chemical properties of an agent, and results from short-term tests, allow a transfer from Group C to B2 or from Group D to C.

Group D—Not Classified

There is inadequate animal evidence of carcinogenicity. Inadequate evidence indicates that because of major qualitative or quantitative limitations, the studies cannot be interpreted as showing either the presence or absence of a carcinogenic effect.

Group E—No Evidence of Carcinogenicity for Humans

There is no evidence of carcinogenicity in at least two adequate animal tests in different species or in both epidemiological and animal studies.

In 1980, OSHA published its general policy for the identification, classification, and regulation of potential occupational carcinogens (OSHA, 1980). This policy evolved from an extensive hearing process involving the testimony of many experts in the field of carcinogenesis. These experts came from leadership positions in government, academia, industry, and international bodies. Regarding the issue of whether or not there are nonzero thresholds for carcinogens, OSHA concluded that presently there is no acceptable way to reliably determine a threshold for a carcinogen. Several other national agencies (FDA, EPA, CPSC,NAS, OSTP) have published identical conclusions (IRLG, 1979; USEPA, 1985; OSTP, 1985; NAS, 1977; FDA, 1979).

There is an additional issue related to the question of carcinogens and thresholds. The distinction between genetic and epigenetic carcinogens is being made by some people. A genetic carcinogen is one which presumably interacts with DNA and has a zero threshold, whereas an epigenetic carcinogen is one which presumably does not interact with DNA and has a nonzero threshold of response. This distinction has been criticized on the basis that there is no firm scientific evidence that epigenetic carcinogens represent less of a hazard than genotoxic carcinogens (Theiss, 1983). However, others feel there is a "substantial" scientific basis for categorizing carcinogens according to their mechanisms (Rodricks and Taylor, 1983). Examples of proposed nongenotoxic (epigenetic) carcinogens include hormones such as estrogens, tumor promoters, and solid-state carcinogens such as implanted metal and plastic (Rodricks and Taylor, 1983). Current regulatory policy in the United States considers all carcinogens to be genotoxic (Rodricks and Taylor, 1983; USEPA, 1985).

A final issue concerns initiators and promoters. Federal regulatory agencies do not distinguish between initiators and promoters, because it is very difficult to confirm that a given chemical acts by promotion alone (OSTP, 1985; OSHA, 1980; USEPA, 1984). A *promoter* is defined as an agent which results in an increase in cancer induction when it is administered some time after the animal has been exposed to an *initiator*. A *cocarcinogen* differs from a promoter only in that it is administered at the same time as the initiator. Initiators, cocarcinogens, and promoters do not usually induce tumors when administered separately. *Complete* carcinogens act as both initiator and promoter (OSTP, 1985). The initiator-promoter model may or may not be valid in general. Some known promoters also have weak tumorigenic activity and some also are initiators. Carcinogens may act as promoters at some tissue sites and initiators at others (OSTP, 1985). Thus far, the initiator-promoter model has been shown to apply only to skin cancer in certain strains of mice. Its applicability to other types of cancer and to humans has not been demonstrated (OSHA, 1980).

The consensus of scientific opinion is that all carcinogens should be assumed to be genotoxic and have a zero threshold dose-response relationship. Thus, the risk analysis method should be used to establish acceptable concentrations for air, water, and food.

3.6.2 Germ-Cell Mutagens

A mutagen is a chemical that can induce alterations in the DNA of either somatic or germinal cells. Mutations carried in germ cells are heritable and may contribute to genetic disease, whereas mutations occurring in somatic cells may be implicated in the etiology of cancer. The use of short-term mutagenicity test results in the interpretation of human carcinogenic risk was mentioned in Section 3.6.1. This section will concentrate on germ-cell mutagenesis.

There are several mutagenic end points of concern. These include point mutations (submicroscopic changes in the base sequence of DNA) and structural or numerical chromosome aberrations. Structural aberrations include deficiencies, duplications, inversions, and translocations. Numerical aberrations are gains or losses of whole chromosomes (trisomy, monosomy) or sets of chromosomes (aneuploidy). Mutagenic effects may also result from mechanisms other than chemical alterations of DNA. Among these are interference with normal DNA synthesis, or induction of DNA misrepair, DNA methylation, abnormal nuclear division processes, or interactions with non-DNA targets, e.g., protamine and tubulin (USEPA, 1984).

There are many test systems available that can contribute information about the mutagenic potential of a chemical. Test systems for detecting point mutations include those in bacteria, eukaryotic microorganisms, higher plants, insects, mammalian somatic cells in culture, and germinal cells of intact mammals. Test systems for detecting structural chromosome aberrations have been developed in a variety of organisms, including higher plants, insects, fish, birds, and several mammalian species. Many of these assays can be performed *in vitro* or *in vivo* and in either germ or somatic cells. Procedures available for detecting structural chromosome aberrations in mammalian germ cells include measurements of heritable translocations or dominant lethality, as well as direct cytogenetic analyses of germ cells and early embryos in rodents. There are also tests available to detect numerical chromosome changes (aneuploidy) in such organisms as fungi, Drosophila, mammalian cells in culture, and intact mammals (USEPA, 1984).

The test systems mentioned above are not the only ones that will provide evidence of mutagenicity or related DNA effects. This small fraction of available tests was cited to convey the complexity of estimating the human mutational risk from short-term tests.

The USEPA has published proposed guidelines for the classification of the weight of evidence for human germ-cell mutagenicity (USEPA, 1984). This classification of germ-cell mutagens necessitates the exercise of considerable judgment because of the complexity and variety of the available data. Germ-cell mutagens are classified into three groups: sufficient, suggestive, and limited evidence of human germ-cell mutagenicity. (Nonmutagenic test responses, e.g., sister chromatid exchange in germ cells, may be used to elevate a chemical's classification).

Sufficient evidence exists when positive responses are demonstrated in: (a) at least one *in vivo* mammalian germ-cell mutation test, or (b) at least two point mutation tests (at least one in mammalian cells) plus sufficient evidence that the chemical interacts with mammalian germ cells, or (c) at least two structural chromosome aberration tests (at least one in mammalian cells) plus sufficient evidence that the chemical interacts with mammalian germ cells, or (d) at least one gene mutation assay in mammalian cells and one structural chromosome aberration test in mammalian cells and sufficient evidence for chemical interaction with mammalian germ cells.

Suggestive evidence exists in those cases in which there are positive data for both mutagenic activity and evidence for chemical interactions in the gonad, but the evidence is less than sufficient. This category is potentially large and heterogeneous in nature, and ranges from almost sufficient to essentially limited.

Limited evidence denotes a situation in which the evidence is limited to information on mutagenic activity (in other than mammalian germ cells) or to evidence of chemical reactivity in the gonads.

The USEPA assumes that germ-cell mutagens which cause point mutations and/or structural chromosome rearrangements have a zero threshold (USEPA, 1984). Also, the USEPA suggests that the results of short-term mutagenicity tests can be used to estimate human risk in terms of increased genetic disease per generation or per lifetime, or the fractional increase in the assumed spontaneous (background) rate of human mutations (USEPA, 1984). However, there is significant controversy regarding whether or not the results of short-term mutagenesis assays can be extrapolated quantitatively to humans (Hogan and Hoel, 1982). It is recommended that short-term mutagenesis tests be used to assess human risk in qualitative terms rather than quantitative terms.

3.6.3 Developmental Toxicants

Developmental toxicity refers to any adverse effect induced pre- or postnatally, e.g., *in utero* death, malformations, altered fetal or neonatal organ or body weight, and altered postnatal development. The conventional test protocol for detecting developmental toxicity can detect embryo- and fetotoxicity. However, postnatal development is seldom evaluated in routine animal studies (USEPA, 1984).

It is extremely difficult to predict potential human developmental toxicity from the results of animal studies. It is not surprising that the USEPA guidelines for the health assessment of suspect developmental toxicants does not contain a classification of the weight of evidence for human developmental effects (USEPA, 1984).

It is conceivable that during early embryogenesis (organogenesis), a developmental effect can be produced if only a few cells are inhibited or killed by one or a few toxic molecules. This line of reasoning would argue that developmental toxicants have zero thresholds (Freese, 1973).

However, there is significant controversy regarding which method is most appropriate for the extrapolation of the results of animal developmental toxicity studies to humans (Hogan and Hoel, 1982). The USEPA takes the position that, at present, there is no mathematical model generally used for estimating developmental toxicity responses below the experimental dose range. This is due primarily to the lack of understanding of the biological mechanisms underlying developmental toxicity, intra/interspecies differences in the types of developmental effects, the influence of maternal effects, and whether or not a threshold exists below which no effect will be produced by an agent (USEPA, 1984). Hence, the USEPA will continue to use safety factors and margins of safety to regulate developmental toxicants (USEPA, 1984). The margin of safety approach consists of calculating the ratio of the NOEL (no-observable-effect level) derived from the most sensitive species to the estimated human exposure level from all sources. The adequacy of the margin of safety is then considered, based upon quality of data, number of species affected, dose-response relationships, and other factors, such as the benefits of the agent (USEPA, 1984).

3.6.4   Organ/Tissue Toxicants

In an adult organism, the inhibition or death of a few cells usually has no observable effect. Only a large extent of cell death usually causes a toxic effect (Freese, 1973). This line of reasoning would argue that organ/tissue toxicants have nonzero thresholds. However, it should be noted that genetic variability in the human population may cause some individuals to have a threshold of response close to zero.

3.6.5   Summary

There are four types of toxicity data that can be used quantitatively and/or qualitatively in the calculation of acceptable air, water, and food concentrations.

- Cancer data (USEPA Groups A-C, Section 3.6.1) can be used *quantitatively* to establish acceptable concentrations based on the risk analysis method. Somatic cell mutation data can be used qualitatively to classify a chemical regarding its potential human carcinogenicity.
- Germ-cell mutation data can be used *qualitatively* to classify a chemical regarding its genetic disease potential.
- Developmental effects data can be used *quantitatively* to establish acceptable concentrations based on the safety factor method.
- Organ/tissue effects data can be used *quantitatively* to establish acceptable concentrations based on the safety factor method.

Sometimes a chemical will produce multiple types of health effects. Whenever both dose-response models (threshold and nonthreshold) apply to a single chemical, the lowest acceptable concentration (calculated from either the safety factor or risk analysis method, Chapter 6) is recommended for adoption.

3.7   DATA BASES

Ideally, acceptable concentrations should be set at levels which prevent the occurrence of immediate and delayed health effects. Examples of immediate effects include changes in the parameters of pulmonary function, mucous membrane irritation, gastrointestinal distress, gross organ/tissue damage, and death. Examples of delayed effects include cancer, genetic disease, developmental effects, and organ/tissue pathologies. If acceptable concentrations are designed to prevent delayed effects, they will almost certainly prevent immediate effects.

The ideal data base for establishing an acceptable concentration would include micro- and macroscopic assessment of cancer, hereditary (genetic) disease, developmental effects, and organ/tissue effects in humans. However, complete human data are rarely available.

3.7.1 Threshold Limit Values and Permissible Exposure Limits

The American Conference of Governmental Industrial Hygienists (ACGIH) publishes guidelines for occupational exposure to airborne contaminants. These guidelines are referred to as threshold limit values (TLVs) and represent the average concentration (in mg/m^3) for an 8-hour workday and a 40-hour workweek to which nearly all workers may be repeatedly exposed, day after day, without adverse effect. TLVs have been established for approximately 650 substances. The protection conferred by TLVs is elusive in that many TLVs (a) are based on anecdotal information, (b) were established to prevent immediate effects, (c) are based on lethal animal dose and short-term no-observable-effect level (NOEL-short term) data, and (d) have not been updated recently. Indeed, the ACGIH state that TLVs are not intended to be used as a relative index of hazard or toxicity or in the evaluation of community air pollution (ACGIH, 1984–85). Hence, the degree of protection against cancer, genetic disease, developmental effects, and organ/tissue pathologies is uncertain with TLVs. TLVs are recommended guidelines and are not enforceable.

Permissible exposure limits (PELs) are enforced by the Occupational Safety and Health Administration. Values for TLVs and PELs are usually close. All of the above criticisms of TLVs also hold for PELs. TLVs and PELs are not recommended for use in establishing acceptable concentrations.

3.7.2. Human Data

Human data from epidemiology studies can have several deficiencies. Conditions of exposure (concentration and time) are usually unknown. End points of toxicity are usually reported only in terms of cause of death. Histopathological examination is rarely included in the study. Hence, much relevant pathology information may be overlooked. Also, it is important to note that epidemiology data reported in terms of proportionate mortality are inappropriate for calculating acceptable concentrations. For a complete discussion of problems associated with the results of proportionate epidemiology studies, see DeCoufle et al., 1980; Najarian, 1978; Walrath and Fraumeni, 1983; and Wong, 1983.

3.7.3 Animal Data

Regarding cancer, the IARC has stated a policy for which there is consensus: "In the absence of adequate data on humans, it is reasonable to regard chemicals for which there is sufficient evidence of carcinogenicity in animals as if they presented a carcinogenic risk to humans" (IARC, 1984). Several federal agencies have either adopted this policy or enunciated one which is very similar: EPA, OSHA, FDA, CPSC, OTA, OSTP, and NAS (USEPA, 1984; IRLG, 1979; OSTP, 1985; OSHA, 1980; OTA, 1977; NAS, 1977; FDA, 1979).

In extrapolating from animals to humans, the doses used in animal bioassays must be adjusted for numerous interspecies differences: body weight, body surface area, lifespan, pharmacokinetics, metabolism, genetic constitution, repair mechanisms, rate of intake, nutritional conditions, bacterial flora, mode/route of exposure, exposure schedule, and competing causes of death (IRLG, 1979; USEPA, 1984). At present, there is no method available to account for all of these differences. Several methods currently used provide incomplete adjustment. These methods assume that animal and human risks are equivalent when exposure is expressed in units of parts per million (ppm) of air, food, or water or when dose rate is expressed in units of milligrams per kilogram of body weight per day (mg/kg/d), milligrams per square meter of body surface per day (mg/m^2/d), or milligrams per kilogram of body weight per lifetime (mg/kg/lifetime) (NRC, 1983). While it is universally recognized that these four exposure/dose rate scales are at best a crude attempt to adjust for many sources of interspecies differences, it appears that the best agreement between observed and predicted human risk is often obtained when a mg/kg/day or a mg/m^2/day dose rate scale is employed (OSTP, 1985).

3.7.4 Units of Dose Rate

Human and animal dose rates are frequently reported in terms of the following abbreviations: NOEL, NOAEL, and LOAEL. These abbreviations are defined as follows (Dourson, 1983):

NOEL   (mg/kg body weight/day) = *no*-observed-effect level. NOEL refers to that dose rate of chemical at which there *are no* statistically or biologically significant increases in frequency or severity of *effects* between the exposed and control groups.

NOAEL (mg/kg body weight/day) = *no*-observed-adverse-effect level. NOAEL refers to that dose rate of chemical at which there *are no* statistically or biologically significant increases in frequency or severity of *adverse effects* between the exposed and control groups. Statistically significant effects are observed at this level, but they are not considered to be adverse.

LOAEL (mg/kg body weight/day) = *lowest*-observed-adverse-effect level. LOAEL refers to that dose rate of chemical at which there *are* statistically or biologically significant increases in frequency or severity of *adverse effects* between the exposed and control groups.

It should be carefully noted that NOELs, NOAELs, and LOAELs must be defined by the period of exposure and period of observation from first and last exposure. Of course, the most relevant type of exposure and observation period for calculating acceptable concentrations are low-level repeated and lifetime, respectively, since delayed effects are of primary concern.

3.7.5 Hierarchy of Data Selection

As discussed in section 3.6, there are two methods for calculating acceptable concentrations: the safety factor method and the risk analysis method. Each method involves different data bases. The safety factor method utilizes, in order of preference, NOEL, NOAEL, or LOAEL data, whereas the risk analysis method utilizes response probability and LOAEL data. Only human or animal studies involving chronic exposure should be used in either method. Chronic exposure refers to low-level repeated or continuous exposure. This is the type of exposure most relevant to the calculation of acceptable concentrations. Both methods should utilize human and animal data in the following order of preference and/or availability:

1. Human data: *lifetime exposure* via the more appropriate route (inhalation or oral)
2. Human data: *less-than-lifetime exposure* with lifetime observation (exposure via the more appropriate route)
3. Human data: *less-than-lifetime exposure* with less-than-lifetime observation (exposure via the more appropriate route)
4. Human data: *lifetime exposure* via the less appropriate route if reasonable toxicologically
5. Human data: *less-than-lifetime exposure* with lifetime observation (exposure via the less appropriate route)
6. Human data: *less-than-lifetime exposure* with less-than-lifetime observation (exposure via the less appropriate route)
7–12. Animal data: same sequence as for human data. Animal studies of

less than 90 days of exposure and/or less than 18 months of observation from first exposure should not be used.

Acceptable concentrations derived from human or animal studies of less-than-lifetime exposure should be referred to as "provisional" acceptable concentrations.

3.8 SUMMARY

The following is a summary list of all the types of information which, ideally, should be derived from an animal or human study in order to carry out a complete risk assessment.

- conditions of exposure (route, concentration, time, and rate of intake)
- body weight
- latent periods (minimum, median, maximum)
- time of observation from first and last exposure
- remaining lifetime from last exposure
- initial number of exposed subjects
- number of subjects surviving at least as long as the minimum latent period from first exposure
- number of cases observed in the exposed group
- number of cases observed in the control group or expected in the exposed group
- median age at first exposure
- type of pathology
- characterization of the control group
- race or species and strain
- sex
- metabolism and pharmacokinetics in animals
- deficiencies in matching among the test, control, and risk groups (e.g. age, smoking habits, exposure to other toxicants)

CHAPTER 4

Quantitative Evaluation of Human and Animal Studies

W. H. Hallenbeck

The first step in the quantitative evaluation of human and animal studies is the calculation of the experimental dose. Note that even if the experimental subjects are animals, the equivalent human experimental dose can be computed. Regardless of whether the experimental subjects are animals or humans, the experimental dose is referred to as the human dose in this book. This designation serves to remind the reader that the calculated experimental dose has been adjusted, if necessary, for inter-species differences in lifetime, latency, body weight, and daily intake of toxicant. It is desirable that the risk group and experimental group doses are as close as possible in terms of magnitude, route, and exposure schedule. (The calculation of risk group dose is discussed in Chapter 5.)

All the other calculations in Chapter 4 involve response. Once the test and control group responses have been calculated, the difference between them is assessed for statistical significance. A study is most useful if the difference between the test and control group responses is statistically significant. Finally, the test group response is adjusted for the control group response. If there is sufficient reason, such as a small sample size or improper control group, the upper limit of the control-adjusted test group response should be computed and used in the risk assessment.

4.1 CALCULATION OF HUMAN DOSE FROM ANIMAL AND HUMAN STUDIES

Always select the highest NOEL/NOAEL or lowest LOAEL from a study of the most sensitive animal species when human data are not available. This practice is necessary because sometimes, as in the case of thalidomide, even the most sensitive animal species tested was less sensitive than humans (Brown and Fabro, 1983). NOEL, NOAEL, and LOAEL can be calculated from animal and human studies as follows:

$$(\text{NOEL, NOAEL, or LOAEL}) = C_j \cdot I_j / W_j \qquad (4.1)$$

where NOEL, NOAEL, or LOAEL are in mg/kg/day
C_j = concentration in mg per unit of contaminated media (air, water, or food)
I_j = intake in units of contaminated media per day (see Tables 4.1-4.3)
W_j = adult body weight in kg (see Table 4.1)
j = 1 refers to data derived from an animal study
j = 2 refers to data derived from a human study

The following conversions of concentration are useful:

ppm = parts per million
1 mg/ℓ(water) = 1 ppm (water)
1 mg/kg(food) = 1 ppm(food)
mg/kg(food) = [mg/kg (body weight)/day] · W_j/I_j
mg/m³(air) = ppm(air) · M / 24.45

where   M = molecular weight of a toxicant (gas)
24.45 = volume in liters of one mole of gas at 25°C and one atmosphere

The ideal study on which to base acceptable concentrations of human exposure would have the following characteristics:

• most sensitive human subjects
• lifetime exposure
• lifetime observation in order to observe delayed effects
• appropriate route of exposure

Very few human studies involve lifetime exposure, and of course animal studies, by definition, are not ideal. Most human and animal studies contain multiple sources of uncertainty. Hence, NOEL, NOAEL, and LOAEL must be adjusted using arbitrary safety factors:

Table 4.1.   Reference Values for Dose Calculations: Lifespan, Body Weight, Food and Water Intake, and Nominal Air Intake for Adults

Species	Sex	Lifespan (yr)	Body Weight (kg)	Food Intake (Wet Weight) (g/day)	Water Intake (mℓ/day)	Air Intake (m³/day)
Human	M	70[a]	75[b]	1500[b,c]	2500[b,c]	20[d]
	F	78[a]	60[b]	1500[b,c]	2500[b,c]	20[d]
Mouse	M	2[c,e]	0.03[e]	5[c]	5[c]	0.04[c,e,f]
	F	2[c,e]	0.025[e]	5[c]	5[c]	0.04[c,e,f]
Rat	M	2[c,e]	0.5[e]	20[e]	25[c,e]	0.2[c,g]
	F	2[c,e]	0.35[e]	18[e]	20[e]	0.2[c,g]
Hamster	M	2[c,e]	0.125[e]	12[e]	15[e]	0.09[e]
	F	2[c,e]	0.110[e]	12[e]	15[e]	0.09[e]

[a]USDOC, 1981.
[b]ICRP, 1975.
[c]Crouch, 1979.
[d]See Tables 4.2 and 4.3 for more exact values.
[e]Gold, 1984.
[f]For more exact values, use: m3/day (mouse) = $0.0345 \, (W/0.025)^{2/3}$, where W = body weight in kg (USEPA, 1980).
[g]For more exact values, use: m3/day (rat) = $0.105 \, (W/0.113)^{2/3}$, where W = body weight in kg (USEPA, 1980).

Table 4.2.   Reference Values for Dose Calculations: Selected Lung Ventilation Values for Humans (ℓ/min)[a]

	Resting (ℓ/min)	Light Activity (ℓ/min)	Heavy Work (ℓ/min)
Male (adult)	7.5	20	43
Female (adult)	6	19	25
Adolescent (14–16 yr)			
Male	5.2		
Female	4.5		
Child (10 yr)	4.8	13	
Infant (1 yr)	1.5	4.2	
Newborn	0.5	1.5	

[a]ICRP, 1975.

Table 4.3.   Reference Values for Dose Calculations: Selected Lung Ventilation Values for Humans (m³ per time period)[a]

	Resting (m³/8 hr)	Light Activity (m³/16 hr)	Light Activity (m³/8 hr)	Heavy Activity (m³/8 hr)	Total (m³/24 hr)
Male (adult)	3.6	19.2			22.8
Male (adult)	3.6		9.6	20.6	33.8
Female (adult)	2.9	18.2			21.1
Female (adult)	2.9		9.1	12	24

[a]ICRP, 1975.

$$(NOEL_a, NOAEL_a, \text{ or } LOAEL_a)$$

$$= (NOEL, NOAEL, \text{ or } LOAEL) / \prod_{i=1}^{n} F_i \qquad (4.2)$$

where a = subscript denoting adjusted data
       n = number of sources of uncertainty
       F_i = one of n safety factors. It is common practice to set the upper limit of the value of an uncertainty factor at 10 (USEPA, 1985).

$$\prod_{i=1}^{n} F_i = F_1 \cdot F_2 \cdot F_3 \cdots F_n$$

The following is a list of recommended safety factors:

F_1 = 1 to 10   to adjust for potential intraspecies variation in sensitivity (USEPA, 1985)

F_2 = 1 to 10   to adjust for potential synergism (USEPA, 1985)

F_3 = 1 to 10   when using an NOEL, NOAEL, or LOAEL based on a less appropriate route (inhalation or oral) (USEPA, 1985)

F_4 = some factor   to adjust for the fraction of total intake of toxicant via the media of interest. For example, in the absence of data to the contrary, assume that drinking water contributes 20% of the daily intake of organic chemicals and therefore F_4 = 5 (USEPA, 1985). IMPORTANT: F_4 is used *only* in the calculation of *acceptable concentrations* using either the risk analysis or safety factor methods (Chapter 6).

F_5 = 1 or 10 F_5 = 1 in risk analysis. F_5 = 10 when using a LOAEL instead of a NOEL or NOAEL in the safety factor method for calculating acceptable concentration (USEPA, 1985).

F_6 = 1 or 10   to adjust for potential interspecies variation in sensitivity (USEPA, 1985). F_6 = 1 for human data. F_6 = 10 for animal data.

Adjustments may also be used to compensate for the sources of error or uncertainty discussed in Chapter 3. These sources include deficiencies in:

• matching between the controls and exposed experimental subjects (Section 3.1)
• latency adjustments and followup periods (Section 3.2)
• matching between the experimental groups and the risk group (Section 3.3)

- quality of the animal study (Section 3.4)
- quality of the epidemiological study (Section 3.5)

Rodent studies involving less than three months of exposure and/or less than 18 months of observation from first exposure are not recommended. Acceptable concentrations calculated on the basis of less-than-lifetime exposure studies should be referred to as "provisional acceptable concentrations" (USEPA, 1985).

Once the NOEL, NOAEL, or LOAEL has been adjusted, the human dose can be calculated from animal and human studies as follows:

$$D_j = \frac{C_j \cdot I_j}{W_j \prod_{i=1}^{n} F_i} \cdot 70 \cdot \frac{T_j}{E_j - L_j} \cdot (74 - L) \cdot 365 \tag{4.3}$$

where D_j = human dose in mg
j = 1 for animal data
j = 2 for human data

C_j, W_j, I_j, and $\prod_{i=1}^{n} F_i$ are defined as in Equations 4.1 and 4.2. $NOEL_a$, $NOAEL_a$ or $LOAEL_a$ may be substituted for

$$[C_j \cdot I_j/(W_j \prod_{i=1}^{n} F_i)]$$

70 = adult human body weight in kg
E_j = lifetime in years
L_j = median latent period in years. Latent period is the time between first exposure and the recognition of response in a subject (see Section 3.2).
L = median human latent period in years
74 = human lifetime in years
365 = days per year
T_j = median exposure time in years, adjusted, if necessary, for latency, remaining lifetime from last exposure, and observation time from last exposure

For data derived from an animal study:

$$D_1 = \frac{C_1 \cdot I_1}{W_1 \prod_{i=1}^{6} F_i} \cdot 70 \cdot \frac{T_1}{E_1 - L_1} \cdot (74 - L) \cdot 365 \tag{4.4}$$

For data derived from a human study:

$$D_2 = \frac{C_2 \cdot I_2}{\prod\limits_{i=1}^{5} F_i} \cdot T_2 \cdot 365 \tag{4.5}$$

since $W_2 = 70$ and $(E_2 - L_2) = (74 - L)$.

4.2 QUANTITATION OF RESPONSE

The frequencies of response in the test and control groups in animal studies can be computed as follows:

$$P_t = X_t/N_t \tag{4.6}$$

$$P_c = X_c/N_c \tag{4.7}$$

where t = subscript denoting test group data
   c = subscript denoting control group data
   P = proportion responding adversely
   N = number of subjects at risk = number of subjects surviving to the minimum latent period
   X = number of cases of : (a) one type of pathology (e.g., a specific tumor type), or (b) any type within a class of pathology (e.g., all tumor-bearing animals = TBA). These two definitions obviate multiple counting of animals with multiple types of pathology (e.g., multiple tumor types).

If there is evidence of premature deaths in the test group, the number at risk (N_t) must be adjusted downward when the response is latent. For a latent response, an animal is considered at risk only if it survived from the time of first exposure for a period at least as long as the minimum latent period.

The results of epidemiological studies are reported in seemingly much different terms than those from animal studies. However, the same fundamental quantities of P_t and P_c can be derived from the terms used to summarize the results of epidemiology studies:

   Obs = number of cases observed in the test (exposed) group; identical to X_t for animal studies
   Exp = expected number of cases in the test group; analogous to X_c for animal studies. The value of Exp is usually based on the health experience of a large control (unexposed) group, such as the general population.
   SMR = standard mortality ratio = ratio of observed to expected number of cases

RR = relative risk = ratio of number the incidence of cases in the test group to that of the control group

It is important to note that error due to multiple counting of subjects with multiple types of pathologies can occur in epidemiology data also. Use the same two definitions of number of cases as were given for animal data.

P_t, P_c, N_t, Obs, Exp, RR, and SMR are related as follows:

$$P_t = Obs/N_t \tag{4.8}$$

$$P_c = Exp/N_t \tag{4.9}$$

$$RR = P_t/P_c \tag{4.10}$$

$$SMR = Obs/Exp \tag{4.11}$$

$$RR = SMR = Obs/Exp = P_t/P_c \tag{4.12}$$

where N_t = number at risk in the test group
P_t = proportion responding adversely (response frequency) in the test group; identical to P_t for animal studies
P_c = proportion expected to respond adversely (response frequency) in the test group; analogous to P_c for animal studies. The value of P_c is usually based on the health experience of a large control (unexposed) group such as the general population

Equation 4.12 can be rearranged to yield three equivalent expressions for P_t:

$$P_t = RR \cdot P_c \tag{4.13}$$

$$P_t = SMR \cdot P_c \tag{4.14}$$

$$P_t = Obs \cdot P_c/Exp \tag{4.15}$$

Sometimes it is impossible to calculate P_t and P_c from an epidemiology study because the number in the exposed group (N_t) was not reported. If cancer is the type of pathology under consideration, values for P_c derived for the general population can be obtained from Tables 4.4 and 4.5. Although the values for P_c in these tables are tabulated for age zero, the probabilities of eventually developing or dying from specific cancers at other attained ages are about the same as at age zero (Seidman, 1985). If values for other years are required, they can be estimated from the following equation:

$$P_c = In \cdot E \tag{4.16}$$

where In = incidence or mortality rate for a selected cancer and year (may also be sex and race specific)
E = life expectancy (in years) at birth for a selected year

Table 4.4.   Probability at Birth of Eventually Developing Cancer, U.S.[a]

Site	White Males			White Females		
	1975	1980	1985	1975	1980	1985
All cancer	.303	.336	.369	.339	.350	.361
Buccal cavity and pharynx	.015	.016	.016	.007	.008	.009
Esophagus	.005	.005	.005	.002	.002	.003
Stomach	.012	.012	.012	.009	.008	.008
Colon/rectum	.053	.059	.065	.058	.064	.069
Pancreas	.012	.012	.012	.011	.012	.013
Larynx	.008	.008	.009	.001	.002	.002
Lung	.069	.078	.087	.025	.033	.042
Breast				.096	.099	.102
Uterus				.070	.060	.050
Cervix				.037	.032	.027
Ovary				.015	.015	.015
Prostate	.061	.074	.087			
Testis	.002	.003	.004			
Kidney	.008	.011	.013	.005	.006	.007
Bladder	.025	.029	.032	.010	.011	.012
Melanoma	.006	.009	.013	.006	.009	.011
Thyroid	.002	.002	.002	.005	.005	.005
Leukemia	.012	.012	.012	.010	.009	.009
Lymphoma and multiple myeloma	.016	.018	.002	.016	.018	.020

[a]Seidman et al., 1985.

Table 4.5.   Probability at Birth of Eventually Dying of Cancer, U.S.[a]

Site	White Males			White Females		
	1975	1980	1985	1975	1980	1985
All cancer	.189	.210	.232	.171	.186	.200
Buccal cavity and pharynx	.005	.005	.005	.002	.003	.003
Esophagus	.004	.004	.005	.002	.002	.002
Stomach	.008	.008	.007	.006	.006	.006
Colon/rectum	.024	.027	.029	.029	.030	.031
Pancreas	.010	.010	.011	.009	.011	.012
Larynx	.003	.003	.003	.000	.001	.001
Lung	.058	.068	.078	.018	.026	.034
Breast				.031	.034	.036
Uterus				.010	.009	.009
Ovary				.009	.010	.012
Prostate	.020	.023	.026			
Testis	.001	.000	.000			
Kidney	.004	.005	.005	.003	.003	.003
Bladder	.007	.007	.008	.003	.004	.004
Melanoma	.002	.003	.003	.002	.002	.002
Thyroid	.000	.000	.000	.001	.001	.001
Leukemia	.008	.009	.010	.007	.007	.008
Lymphoma and multiple myeloma	.010	.010	.010	.010	.010	.010

[a]Seidman et al., 1985.

Problem 4.1

What is the probability at birth of eventually developing stomach cancer for white males born in 1975?

Solution to Problem 4.1

The incidence of stomach cancer for U.S. white males was 12.4 per 100,000 in 1975 (adjusted to the 1970 U.S. age distribution) (SEER, 1984), and the life expectancy at birth for U.S. white males was 69.4 years in 1975 (USDOC, 1981). Substitution of these values into Equation 4.16 yields:

$$P_c = 12.4 \cdot 69.4/10^5 = 0.009$$

This value of $P_c = 0.009$ compares favorably with the more accurately calculated value of 0.012 reported in Table 4.4. Equation 4.16 is useful whenever P_c for a selected year cannot be found in the published literature. Seidman et al. (1985) have traced the history of the published literature on P_c.

4.3 TESTS OF SIGNIFICANCE

This discussion will be restricted to the statistical treatment of a dichotomous response variable, i.e., the proportion of subjects responding in the test and control groups. There are three ways to test the statistical significance of the difference between two proportions. One is the Fisher's exact test based on the binomial distribution (Mattson, 1981). This test requires laborious calculations. The normal (Colton, 1974) and Poisson (Hays, 1981) approximations to the binomial distribution can be used whenever certain criteria are satisfied. If these criteria are satisfied, all three probability distributions will yield about the same result. The two approximate methods do not require laborious calculations.

The normal distribution can be used to approximate the binomial distribution whenever each of $N_t p$, $N_t q$, $N_c p$, and $N_c q$ is greater than or equal to five (see below for an explanation of abbreviations). This approximate test consists of calculating the critical ratio which follows the normal distribution:

$$z = (P_t - P_c)/\{pq[(1/N_t) + (1/N_c)]\}^{1/2} \qquad (4.17)$$

where z = critical ratio

$p = (X_t + X_c)/(N_t + N_c)$

$q = 1 - p$

$P_t, P_c, N_t,$ and N_c are defined the same as for Equations 4.6 - 4.9

Problem 4.2

Let $P_t = 20/100 = 0.2$ and $P_c = 6/100 = 0.06$. Is the difference between the test and control group responses statistically significant?

Solution to Problem 4.2

$$
\begin{aligned}
N_t &= N_c = 100 \\
X_t &= 20 \\
X_c &= 6 \\
P_t &= 0.2 \\
P_c &= 0.06 \\
p &= (20 + 6)/(100 + 100) = 0.13 \\
q &= 1 - p = 1 - 0.13 = 0.87 \\
N_t p &= 100 \cdot 0.13 = 13 \\
N_t q &= 100 \cdot 0.87 = 87 \\
N_c p &= 100 \cdot 0.13 = 13 \\
N_c q &= 100 \cdot 0.87 = 87
\end{aligned}
$$

Since each of $N_t p$, $N_t q$, $N_c p$ and $N_c q$ is greater than five, the normal approximation to the binomial can be used to test for the statistical significance of the difference between P_t and P_c:

$$z = (0.2 - 0.06)/\{0.13 \cdot 0.87[(1/100) + (1/100)]\}^{1/2} = 2.94$$

Upon referring this critical ratio to a table of the normal distribution (Table 4.6), the probability due to chance alone that an experiment will produce a difference between P_t and P_c as great or greater than 0.14 ($P_t - P_c = 0.20 - 0.06$) is 0.2%. This probability is abbreviated as P-value = 0.002, and the difference is judged to be statistically significant.

The Poisson approximation to the binomial distribution can be used whenever a proportion is less than or equal to 20% and sample size is greater than or equal to fifty (Hays, 1981). In Problem 4.2, both the test and control responses are less than or equal to 20%, and both sample sizes are greater than 50. Table 4.7 can be used to test the statistical significance of the difference between 20 observed cases in the test group and 6 observed cases in the control group. Entering Table 4.7 at 6 responses, we find that 20 is greater than 14.57 in the 99% column. Hence the probability due to chance alone of observing 20 or more cases,

Table 4.6.   Areas in One Tail of the Standard Normal Curve[a]

z	.00	.01	.02	.03	.04	.05	.06	.07	.08	.09
0.0	.500	.496	.492	.488	.484	.480	.476	.472	.468	.464
0.1	.460	.456	.452	.448	.444	.440	.436	.433	.429	.425
0.2	.421	.417	.413	.409	.405	.401	.397	.394	.390	.386
0.3	.382	.378	.374	.371	.367	.363	.359	.356	.352	.348
0.4	.345	.341	.337	.334	.330	.326	.323	.319	.316	.312
0.5	.309	.305	.302	.298	.295	.291	.288	.284	.281	.278
0.6	.274	.271	.268	.264	.261	.258	.255	.251	.248	.245
0.7	.242	.239	.236	.233	.230	.227	.224	.221	.218	.215
0.8	.212	.209	.206	.203	.200	.198	.195	.192	.189	.187
0.9	.184	.181	.179	.176	.174	.171	.169	.166	.164	.161
1.0	.159	.156	.154	.152	.149	.147	.145	.142	.140	.138
1.1	.136	.133	.131	.129	.127	.125	.123	.121	.119	.117
1.2	.115	.113	.111	.109	.107	.106	.104	.102	.100	.099
1.3	.097	.095	.093	.092	.090	.089	.087	.085	.084	.082
1.4	.081	.079	.078	.076	.075	.074	.072	.071	.069	.068
1.5	.067	.066	.064	.063	.062	.061	.059	.058	.057	.056
1.6	.055	.054	.053	.052	.051	.049	.048	.048	.046	.046
1.7	.045	.044	.043	.042	.041	.040	.039	.038	.038	.037
1.8	.036	.035	.034	.034	.033	.032	.031	.031	.030	.029
1.9	.029	.028	.027	.027	.026	.026	.025	.024	.024	.023
2.0	.023	.022	.022	.021	.021	.020	.020	.019	.019	.018
2.1	.018	.017	.017	.017	.016	.016	.015	.015	.015	.014
2.2	.014	.014	.013	.013	.013	.012	.012	.012	.011	.011
2.3	.011	.010	.010	.010	.010	.009	.009	.009	.009	.008
2.4	.008	.008	.008	.008	.007	.007	.007	.007	.007	.006
2.5	.006	.006	.006	.006	.006	.005	.005	.005	.005	.005
2.6	.005	.005	.004	.004	.004	.004	.004	.004	.004	.004
2.7	.003	.003	.003	.003	.003	.003	.003	.003	.003	.003
2.8	.003	.002	.002	.002	.002	.002	.002	.002	.002	.002
2.9	.002	.002	.002	.002	.002	.002	.002	.001	.001	.001
3.0	.001									

[a]Colton, 1974.

when 6 are expected, is less than 1%. This probability is abbreviated as P-value < 0.01. In this problem the sample sizes were the same. Whenever they are different, an adjustment must be made such that the observed numbers of cases in the test and control groups are based on the same sample sizes.

Problem 4.3

Let $P_t = 20/100$ and $P_c = 20/200$. Is the difference between the test and control responses statistically significant?

Table 4.7. Limits for a Poisson Variable[a]

Number of Responses, X_c	Lower Limits		Upper Limits	
	1%	5%	95%	99%
0	0.0000	0.0000	3.00	4.61
1	0.0101	0.0513	4.74	6.64
2	0.149	0.355	6.30	8.41
3	0.436	0.818	7.75	10.05
4	0.823	1.37	9.15	11.60
5	1.28	1.97	10.51	13.11
6	1.79	2.61	11.84	14.57
7	2.33	3.29	13.15	16.00
8	2.91	3.98	14.43	17.40
9	3.51	4.70	15.71	18.78
10	4.13	5.43	16.96	20.14
11	4.77	6.17	18.21	21.49
12	5.43	6.92	19.44	22.82
13	6.10	7.69	20.67	24.14
14	6.78	8.46	21.89	25.45
15	7.48	9.25	23.10	26.74
16	8.18	10.04	24.30	28.03
17	8.89	10.83	25.50	29.31
18	9.62	11.63	26.69	30.58
19	10.35	12.44	27.88	31.85
20	11.08	13.25	29.06	33.10
21	11.82	14.07	30.24	34.36
22	12.57	14.89	31.42	35.60
23	13.33	15.72	32.59	36.84
24	14.09	16.55	33.75	38.08
25	14.85	17.38	34.92	39.31
26	15.62	18.22	36.08	40.53
27	16.40	19.06	37.23	41.76
28	17.17	19.90	38.39	42.98
29	17.96	20.75	39.54	44.19
30	18.74	21.59	40.69	45.40
35	22.72	25.87	46.40	51.41
40	26.77	30.20	52.07	57.35
45	30.88	34.56	57.69	63.23
50	35.03	38.96	63.29	69.07

[a]Pearson and Hartley, 1966.

Solution to Problem 4.3

The Poisson distribution can be used to approximate a P-value for the difference between X_c and X_t. X_c or X_t must be adjusted to the same sample size. Always make the adjustment on the basis of the smaller sample size:

$$X_c = 20 \cdot 100/200 = 10$$

Table 4.7 can be used to test the statistical significance of the difference between 20 cases in the test group and 10 cases in the control group.

Entering Table 4.7 at 10 responses, we find that 20 is greater than 16.96 and less than 20.14. Hence, the probability due to chance alone of observing 20 or more cases, when 10 are expected, is less than 5% and greater than 1%. This probability is abbreviated as $0.01 <$ P-value < 0.05.

Several important questions arise regarding the statistical treatment of tumor incidence data from animal studies. These questions involve the distinction between benign and malignant tumors, the relevance of certain tumor types to humans, and the statistical treatment of multiple tumor types in the same animal.

Benign and malignant tumors should be viewed as being equally serious. Few, if any, tumor types are presently known to stop at the benign stage and never evolve to the invasive and metastasizing stage of malignancy (IRLG, 1979). Hence, statistical analyses of data should treat animals with benign or malignant neoplasms in the same manner. That sites of tumors may vary among species for a given chemical does not diminish the significance of a positive finding in any one species. There are many examples where the target sites are the same or different between animals and humans (IRLG, 1979). Therefore, it is appropriate to base a risk analysis on animal tumor data (benign or malignant) unless the type of animal tumor is one that has never appeared in humans either spontaneously or by induction.

Sometimes the results of animal studies are complicated by the occurrence of multiple tumor types in the same animal. These multiple tumor types could represent multiple primary or secondary (metastasized) tumors. A problem arises when the total risk is computed by summing the risks due to each type of tumor. Clearly, the total risk could exceed 100% because of multiple inclusion of the same animal in the computation of individual tumor risks. As discussed above, all animal tumor types are likely to be relevant to humans. Hence, a better method of computing the overall tumor risk consists of dividing the number of tumor-bearing animals (TBA) by the total number at risk. The number at risk consists of all animals surviving from the time of first exposure for a period at least as long as the median latent period.

When the overall tumor response in the test group is not statistically significantly greater than that in the control group, further data analysis may be necessary. Frequently, one or more individual tumor types will be statistically significant. Risk assessment can then proceed on the basis of individual tumor types rather than on overall tumor types. It is usually best to proceed using the single highest tumor response rate, because as the number of significant individual tumor types increases so does the potential for error due to multiple inclusion of the same animal.

4.4 CALCULATION OF CONTROL-ADJUSTED TEST GROUP RESPONSE

In most human or animal studies, a naturally occurring background or control response will be observed. There are three biological models which can be used to describe the interaction between control and test-dose responses (Hoel, 1980).

The first model assumes that the mechanism of control response is identical (i.e., additive) to that of the test dose response:

$$P_e = P_t - P_c \qquad (4.18)$$

where P_e = control-adjusted test group response (due to the test-dose alone)
     = excess risk due to the test dose alone
     P_t and P_c are defined the same as for Equations 4.6 – 4.9

The second model assumes that the mechanism of control response is completely different from (i.e., independent of) that of the test dose response. Abbott's correction yields a mathematical description of the second model:

$$P_e = (P_t - P_c)/(1 - P_c) \qquad (4.19)$$

The third model assumes that the control response is caused by both additive and independent mechanisms:

$$P_e = (P_t - P_c)/(1 - a\,P_c) \qquad (4.20)$$

where a = proportion of control response caused by an independent mechanism

Equation 4.20 is a generalization of Equations 4.18 and 4.19. For the case of complete additivity of mechanisms, a = 0, and Equation 4.20 reduces to Equation 4.18. For the case of complete independence of mechanisms, a = 1, and Equation 4.20 reduces to Equation 4.19.

In general, the proportion of control response caused by an independent mechanism is unknown. Hence, the choice is between using Equations 4.18 and 4.19. Since Equation 4.19 will yield the more conservative result, i.e., the higher risk for a given dose, it will be used to calculate control-adjusted test group response in this book.

It is very important to completely characterize P_e in order to assess its relevance to a human risk group (general population or workers). A complete description of P_e would include specification of the following:

• type of pathology
• race or species and strain and sex
• conditions of exposure (route, dose, dose rate)

- observation time from the first and last exposure
- age at first exposure
- latent period (minimum, median, maximum)
- nature of the control group

4.5 CALCULATION OF THE UPPER LIMIT OF CONTROL-ADJUSTED TEST GROUP RESPONSE

This discussion will be restricted to the statistical treatment of a dichotomous response variable, i.e., proportion of subjects responding in the test and control groups. Hence, the cumulative binomial probability distribution is assumed to be the most appropriate mathematical model. Calculations involving the cumulative binomial distribution usually necessitate a computer. Solutions for sample sizes up to 200 are tabulated in Appendix 1. For sample sizes which exceed 200, the Poisson and normal approximations to the binomial distribution can be used when certain criteria are satisfied. If these criteria are satisfied, all three probability distributions will yield about the same solution for the upper limit of response due to the test dose alone.

The best way to understand the use of the binomial, Poisson, and normal distributions in the calculations of response limits is to systematically work through example problems. Two examples will be presented, one involving animal data and the other epidemiology data. Although not readily apparent, animal and epidemiology data present identical mathematical challenges which entail identical solutions.

Problem 4.4

Given the following experimental animal data, calculate the upper 99% limit of response due to the test dose alone (the difference between P_t and P_c is statistically significant with a P-value = 0.002):

$$P_t = X_t/N_t = 20/100 = 0.20$$
$$P_c = X_c/N_c = 6/100 = 0.06$$

Solution to Problem 4.4

The response due to the test dose alone can be calculated from Equation 4.19:

$$P_e = (P_t - P_c)/(1 - P_c)$$
$$= (0.2 - 0.06)/(1 - 0.06) = 0.15$$

A modification of Equation 4.19 can be used to calculate the upper limit of response due to the test dose alone:

$$P'_e = (P'_t - P'_c)/(1 - P'_c) \qquad (4.21)$$

where P'_e = upper limit of control-adjusted test group response
P'_t = upper limit of test group response
P'_c = lower limit of control group response

From Appendix 1, values based on the cumulative binomial distribution can be obtained for the upper 99% limit of P_t and the lower 1% limit of P_c:

$$P'_t(99\%) = 0.31$$

$$P'_c(1\%) = 0.02$$

The solution of $P'_t(99\%) = 0.31$ means that the true test group response could be as high as 0.31, with one experiment out of 100 yielding 20 or fewer responses. Note that $P'_t(99\%) = 0.31$ is about 50% greater than $P_t = 0.20$. The solution of $P'_c(1\%) = 0.02$ means that the true control group response could be as low as 0.02 with one experiment out of 100 yielding 6 or more responses. Note that $P'_c(1\%) = 0.02$ is one-third of $P_c = 0.06$.

Substitution of $P'_t(99\%)$ and $P'_c(1\%)$ into Equation 4.21 yields a solution for the upper 99% limit of response due to the test dose alone:

$$P'_e(99\%) = (0.31 - 0.02)/(1 - 0.02) = 0.30$$

Note that $P'_e(99\%) = 0.30$ is twice $P_e = 0.15$. The meaning of $P'_e(99\%) = 0.30$ is that there is a 99% probability that the true value of P_e is less than or equal to 0.30.

The Poisson or normal approximations to the binomial distribution must be used whenever the sample size exceeds 200 and/or some other upper limit of test dose response is desired, e.g., the upper 95% limit. This is because Appendix 1 contains only upper 99% limits and lower 1% limits for sample sizes up to 200.

The Poisson distribution can be used to approximate the binomial distribution whenever a response is less than or equal to 20% and sample size is greater than or equal to 50 (Hays, 1981). In Problem 4.4, both the test and control responses are less than or equal to 20%, and both sample sizes are greater than 50. Hence, the Poisson approximation to the binomial can be used. The value $P'_t(99\%) = 0.33$ can be obtained from Table 4.7 as follows: for $X_t = 20$, the entry of 33.1 can be found under the upper 99% limit column; 33.1 is then divided by $N_t = 100$ to obtain $P'_t(99\%) = 0.33$. Note that this result is quite close to that obtained using the binomial distribution. The value $P'_c(1\%) = 0.02$ can be obtained from Table 4.7 as follows: for $X_c = 6$, the entry of 1.79 can be found under the lower 1% limit column; 1.79 is then divided by $N_c = 100$ to obtain $P'_c(1\%) = 0.02$. Note that this result is identical to that obtained using the binomial distribution. The 95% upper and 5% lower limits should be used whenever $P'_t(95\%)$ and $P'_c(5\%)$ are required.

Substitution of $P'_t(99\%)$ and $P'_c(1\%)$ into Equation 4.21 yields about the same solution for $P'_e(99\%)$ as before:

$$P'_e(99\%) = (0.33 - 0.02)/(1 - 0.02) = 0.32$$

The normal distribution can be used to approximate the binomial distribution whenever each of N_tP_t, N_tQ_t, N_cP_c, and N_cQ_c is greater than or equal to 5 ($Q_t = 1 - P_t$ and $Q_c = 1 - P_c$). In Problem 4.4, $N_tP_t = 20$, $N_tQ_t = 80$, $N_cP_c = 6$, and $N_cQ_c = 94$. Hence, the normal approximation to the binomial can be used. Since the Poisson approximation requires minimal computations, the normal approximation should be resorted to only when the criteria for using the Poisson are not satisfied.

P'_t and P'_c can be calculated from the normal distribution as follows:

$$P'_t = P_t + z (P_tQ_t/N_t)^{1/2} \tag{4.22}$$

$$P'_c = P_c - z (P_cQ_c/N_c)^{1/2} \tag{4.23}$$

where z = the critical ratio at upper and lower cumulative probabilities

For Problem 4.4,

$$P'_t(99\%) = 0.2 + 2.326(0.2 \times 0.8/100)^{1/2} = 0.29$$

$$P'_c(1\%) = 0.06 - 2.326(0.06 \times 0.94/100)^{1/2} = 0.005$$

Substitution of $P'_t(99\%)$ and $P'_c(1\%)$ into Equation 4.21 yields about the same solution for $P'_e(99\%)$ as before:

$$P'_e(99\%) = (0.29 - 0.005)/(1 - 0.005) = 0.29$$

Problem 4.5

Given the following epidemiological data, calculate the upper 99% limit of response due to the test dose alone (the difference between observed and expected is statistically significant with a P-value < 0.01):

$$Obs = 15$$

$$Exp = 5$$

$$N_t = N_c = 1000$$

Solution to Problem 4.5

From Equation 4.8 and 4.9:

$$P_t = Obs/N_t = 15/1000 = 0.015$$

$$P_c = Exp/N_t = 5/1000 = 0.005$$

The response due to test dose alone can be calculated from Equation 4.19:

$$P_e = (0.015 - 0.005)/(1 - 0.005) = 0.01$$

A modification of Equation 4.19 can be used to calculate the upper limit of response due to the test dose alone:

$$P'_e = (P'_t - P_c)/(1 - P_c) \qquad (4.24)$$

Note that values for P_c and Exp in epidemiology studies are usually derived from large control groups such as the general population. Therefore, it is unnecessary to use the lower limit of P_c to calculate P'_e.

Use the Poisson approximation to calculate P'_t, since the sample size of 1000 exceeds the range of Appendix 1 (binomial solutions), and the normal approximation requires more computation. Enter Table 4.7 at 15 responses and obtain 26.74 from the upper 99% limit column. Divide 26.74 by 1000. Hence $P'_t(99\%) = 26.74/1000 = 0.027$. Substitution of $P'_t(99\%)$ into Equation 4.24 yields:

$$P'_e(99\%) = (0.027 - 0.005)/(1 - 0.005) = 0.02$$

Note that $P'_e(99\%) = 0.02$ is twice $P_e = 0.01$.

CHAPTER 5

Risk Analysis

W. H. Hallenbeck and K. M. Cunningham

Risk analysis involves the calculation of individual excess risk, the number of excess cases, and a discussion of the impact of various sources of error (sensitivity analysis). The procedures are relatively unequivocal for risk group (general population or worker) doses which fall within the range of experimental doses derived from animal and/or epidemiology studies. However, most risk group doses fall well below the lowest experimental dose. For toxicants known or assumed to have zero thresholds (e.g., carcinogens), linear interpolation is used to calculate excess risk between the lowest experimental dose and the origin (at zero dose and zero response).

5.1 INDIVIDUAL EXCESS RISK

5.1.1 Experimental Dose Range

When the dose for an individual at risk falls into an experimental dose range, the individual excess risk can be calculated directly from the equation used to fit the experimental dose response data. The general form of this equation is:

$$P = f(D_3) \qquad (5.1)$$

where P = individual excess risk at a certain dose
$f(D_3)$ = some mathematical function of dose (in mg) used to fit experimental dose-response data (i.e., P_e or P'_e vs D_j data)
D_3 = individual dose in mg

$$D_3 = C \cdot I \cdot T_3 \qquad (5.2)$$

where C = concentration in mg per unit of contaminated media (air, water, or food)
I = intake in units of contaminated human media per day (see Tables 4.1–4.3)
T_3 = individual exposure time in days (adjusted, if necessary, for latency and remaining lifetime from last exposure).
If $(E' - L) < 0$, then $T_3 = (T - L + E') \cdot$ (days of exposure/year); if $(E' - L) \geq 0$, then $T_3 = T \cdot$ (days of exposure/year)
E' = remaining lifetime from last exposure (in years)
L = median latent period in years
T = actual exposure time in years

5.1.2 Subexperimental Dose Range

Usually, the dose for an individual at risk is well below the range of experimental doses. In this case, linear interpolation is recommended between the response observed at the lowest experimental dose and the origin (at zero dose and zero response) for toxicants which are known or assumed to have zero thresholds (e.g., carcinogens). The individual excess risk can be calculated as follows:

$$P = R \cdot D_3 = R \cdot C \cdot I \cdot T_3 \qquad (5.3)$$

where P = individual excess risk at a certain dose
R = risk factor (in mg^{-1}) = excess risk per unit of dose (derived from the lowest available experimental dose-response point)
D_3 = individual dose in mg

It is important to review the assumptions underlying Equation 5.3:

• The mechanism of toxicity at the lowest available experimental dose is the same as that for the risk group dose.
• The dose-response relationship below the lowest available experimental dose is well approximated by linear interpolation between the experimental dose and the origin.
• The risk factor derived from an animal or human study is applicable to the risk group.

The risk factor refers to the ratio of the control-adjusted test group response to the human dose derived from an animal or human study:

$$R = P_e/D_j \qquad (5.4)$$

where   R = risk factor in mg^{-1}

P_e = control-adjusted test group response derived from an animal or human study and calculated from Equation 4.19

D_j = lowest effective human dose in mg derived from an animal or human study and calculated from either Equation 4.4 or 4.5

It is very important to completely characterize a risk factor in order to assess its relevance to an individual at risk. A complete description of R would include specification of the following:

- type of pathology
- race or species and strain and sex
- conditions of exposure (route, dose, dose rate)
- observation time from the first and last exposure
- age at first exposure
- latent period (minimum, median, maximum)
- nature of the control group

If there is sufficient reason to suspect that a risk factor has been underestimated, use P'_e in the calculation of R':

$$R' = P'_e/D_j \qquad (5.5)$$

where   R' = upper limit on R, in mg^{-1}

P'_e = upper limit on the control-adjusted test group response, calculated from either Equation 4.21 or 4.24

D_j = same as Equation 5.4

5.1.3 Risk Factor Analysis

Risk factor analysis should be performed in order to evaluate whether a calculated risk may over- or underestimate the true risk. When more than one dose-response data point is available, a trend toward greater or lesser risk per unit of dose can be discerned by making a plot of the risk factors at each dose vs dose. Usually there will be some variation in risk factors due to experimental error alone. If it is not clear from the plot that a trend exists, the data should be analyzed using formal statistical trend analysis.

Two data sets are given in Table 5.1 to illustrate risk factor analysis. Note that in both examples response increases as the dose increases. However, the risk factors decrease with decreasing dose in Example A and increase with decreasing dose in Example B. Example B indicates

Table 5.1.   Risk Factor Data

Response	Dose (mg)	Risk Factor[a]
Example A		
1×10^{-2}	1	1×10^{-2}
6×10^{-2}	2	3×10^{-2}
2.8×10^{-1}	4	7×10^{-2}
5.4×10^{-1}	6	9×10^{-2}
Example B		
1×10^{-2}	1	1×10^{-2}
1.5×10^{-2}	2	7.5×10^{-3}
2×10^{-2}	4	5×10^{-3}
2.4×10^{-2}	6	4×10^{-3}

[a]Risk factor = P_e/D_j.

that the toxicant is more effective per unit of dose in causing the health effect at lower doses than it is at higher doses.

This dose-response dynamic is significant because a risk analysis usually requires the estimation of risks in the subexperimental dose range. Consequently, if risk factor analysis indicates an increasing risk per unit of dose as the dose decreases, a conservative analysis requires the assumption that the trend may continue into the subexperimental dose range.

The risk analysis method presented in this book utilizes linear extrapolation with a fixed risk factor. The value of the risk factor is derived from the lowest significant experimental dose-response data point. If risk factors continue to increase below the lowest experimental dose, an equation based on linear extrapolation may yield an underestimate of risk. Alternatively, if risk factors continue to decrease below the lowest experimental dose, an equation based on linear extrapolation may yield an overestimate of risk.

The rate of change of the risk factor with dose should be examined in the lowest range of experimental data points. Referring to Examples A and B, the slopes for the lowest two data points are, respectively,

$$(3 - 1) \cdot 10^{-2} \text{ mg}^{-1}/\text{mg} = 2 \cdot 10^{-2} \text{ mg}^{-2}$$

$$(0.75 - 1) \cdot 10^{-2} \text{ mg}^{-1}/\text{mg} = -2.5 \cdot 10^{-3} \text{ mg}^{-2}$$

A positive slope indicates that the risk factor *may* continue to decrease below the lowest experimental dose; a negative slope indicates that the risk factor *may* continue to increase below the lowest experimental dose. Depending on the magnitude of the slope and the range of extrapolation, the risk assessor may wish to adjust the risk factor up or down. The adjustment could take the form of an arbitrary adjustment of the risk factor and/or the use of an upper or lower statistical bound on the risk factor, e.g., Equation 5.5.

Often, risks in epidemiological studies are expressed as relative risks. (Relative risk = observed cases/expected cases.) When risks are expressed in this manner it is possible to use the relative risk coefficient (RRC) to analyze relative dose-effectiveness. Relative risk coefficient is defined as follows:

$$\text{RRC} = \frac{(\text{observed cases/expected cases}) - 1}{\text{dose}}$$

An example of an analysis of dose-effectiveness based upon the relative risk coefficient is given in Chapter 8.

5.1.4 Plausibility Analysis

The plausibility of values for excess cancer risk calculated from Equation 5.1 or 5.3 can be assessed by comparison with values in Tables 4.4 and 4.5. Values in these tables represent overall U.S. experience and include the effects of natural and anthropogenic causes of cancer. Although values are tabulated for age zero, the probabilities of eventually developing or dying from specific types of cancer at other attained ages are about the same as at age zero (Seidman, 1985).

If the human exposure is limited to a subset of the general U.S. population or a certain occupationally exposed group, the calculated excess risk added to the overall U.S. experience will exceed the overall U.S. experience tabulated in Tables 4.4 and 4.5. The higher the excess risk, the more likely that an effect would be detected in an epidemiological study. If the calculated value of excess risk is many times that of the overall U.S. experience, the risk analysis may be questionable. However, it is always possible that the risk analysis revealed a heretofore unrecognized source of industrial or general population disease.

5.2 EXCESS CASES

5.2.1 Experimental Dose Range

An important part of risk analysis is the estimation of the number of excess cases which will result from a certain exposure. When the dose for a risk group (general population or worker) falls into an experimental dose range (derived from an animal or human study), the number of excess cases can be calculated as follows:

$$EC = P \cdot N = f(D_4) \cdot N \qquad (5.6)$$

where
- EC = number of excess cases in a risk group
- P = group excess risk at a certain dose
- $f(D_4)$ = some mathematical function of dose (in mg) used to fit experimental dose-response data (i.e., P_e or P'_e vs D_j data)
- N = number of people in a risk group
- D_4 = risk group dose in mg

$$D_4 = C \cdot I \cdot T \qquad (5.7)$$

where
- C = concentration in mg per unit of contaminated media (air, water, or food)
- I = intake in units of contaminated human media per day (see Tables 4.1-4.3)
- T = actual exposure time in days

5.2.2 Subexperimental Dose Range

Usually, the risk group dose is well below the range of experimental doses. In this case, linear interpolation is recommended between the response at the lowest experimental dose and the origin (at zero dose and zero response) for toxicants which are known or assumed to have zero thresholds (e.g., carcinogens). For a risk group of constant size and exposure to one concentration over time, the number of excess cases can be calculated from:

$$EC = P \cdot N = R \cdot D_4 \cdot N = R \cdot C \cdot I \cdot T \cdot N \qquad (5.8)$$

where
- EC = number of excess cases in a risk group
- P = group excess risk at a certain dose
- N = number of people in a risk group
- R (or R') = risk factor (in mg^{-1}) calculated from either Equation 5.4 or 5.5
- D_4 = risk group dose in mg (see Equation 5.7)

A risk group will usually include older individuals who do not have a sufficient life expectancy to manifest a latent effect. Hence, Equations 5.6 and 5.8 will result in an overestimate of excess cases unless N is adjusted downward. However, the possibility of overestimation is reduced because life expectancy increases with increasing attained age (see Table 5.2). Also, it is likely that latent periods decrease with age as defense and repair systems become less efficient. In any case, inclusion of the oldest group (65 years and over) has a relatively small impact on the calculated value of excess cases, since this group comprises only 11% of the general population (see Table 5.3).

Unfortunately, Equation 5.8 is only useful when a risk group of con-

Table 5.2.   U.S. Life Expectancy (All Races, Both Sexes), 1978[a]

Attained Age	Life Expectancy at Attained Age
3	75
7	75
12	75
17	75
22	75
27	76
32	76
37	76
42	77
47	77
52	78
57	79
62	80
65	81

[a]USDOC, 1981.

Table 5.3.   U.S. Age Distribution (all races, both sexes), 1980[a]

Age Group	%
<5	7.2
5–9	7.4
10–14	8.1
15–19	9.3
20–24	9.4
25–29	8.6
30–34	7.8
35–39	6.2
40–44	5.2
45–49	4.9
50–54	5.2
55–59	5.1
60–64	4.5
≥65	11.3

[a]USDOC, 1981.

stant size is exposed to one concentration over time. Equation 5.8 is the simplest case of the following general equation for excess cases when there are multiple combinations of number exposed, exposure concentration, and exposure time:

$$EC = R \cdot I \sum_{i=1}^{k} C_i T_i N_i \qquad (5.9)$$

where i = 1 to k combinations of exposure concentration, exposure time, and
size of risk group

There are three simplified cases of Equation 5.9 besides Case 1 (Equation 5.8):

Case 2. A risk group of constant size is exposed to k combinations of concentration and time.

$$EC = R \cdot I \cdot N \sum_{i=1}^{k} C_i T_i \qquad (5.10)$$

Case 3. Several risk groups are exposed to the same constant concentration for different times.

$$EC = R \cdot I \cdot C \sum_{i=1}^{k} N_i T_i \qquad (5.11)$$

Case 4. Several risk groups are exposed to different concentrations for the same period of time.

$$EC = R \cdot I \cdot T \sum_{i=1}^{k} N_i C_i \qquad (5.12)$$

Problem 5.1

Everyone in a general population risk group of 10,000 people is continuously exposed to 0.01 mg/m³ of an airborne carcinogen for 10 years. How many excess cases of cancer are expected? (Assume N and C are constant over time, $R = 10^{-6}$ mg^{-1}, and $I = 20$ m³/day from Table 4.1.)

Solution to Problem 5.1

Use Equation 5.8, since a risk group of constant size is exposed to one concentration over time:

$$EC = R \cdot C \cdot I \cdot T \cdot N$$

$$= 10^{-6} \text{ mg}^{-1} \cdot 0.01 \text{ mg/m}^3 \cdot 20 \text{ m}^3/\text{d} \cdot 10 \text{ y} \cdot 365 \text{ d/y} \cdot 10^4$$

$$= 7$$

Problem 5.1 could also apply to a worker risk group. Since workers would not be exposed continuously, the values for daily intake and time of exposure would be somewhat different, e.g., $I = 20.6$ m³/day (see Table 4.3) and

$$T = 5 \text{ d/w} \cdot 50 \text{ w/y} \cdot 10y = 250 \text{ days/year} \cdot 10y = 2500 \text{ days}$$

Problem 5.2

General population risk groups are exposed daily to a waterborne carcinogen as follows:

Number	Concentration (mg/ℓ)	Time (years)
1000	5	1
2000	4	2
3000	3	3
4000	2	4
5000	1	5

How many excess cases of cancer are expected? (Assume N_i and C_i are constant over T_i, $R = 10^{-7}$ mg^{-1} and $I = 2.5$ ℓ/day from Table 4.1.)

Solution to Problem 5.2

Use Equation 5.9, since there are multiple combinations of number exposed, exposure concentration, and exposure time:

$$EC = R \cdot I \sum_{i=1}^{k} C_i T_i N_i = 10^{-7} \cdot 2.5 \sum_{i=1}^{5} C_i T_i N_i$$

$$= 10^{-7} \cdot 2.5 \cdot 365(5000 + 16000 + 27000 + 32000 + 25000)$$

$$= 10$$

Problem 5.3

Everyone in a risk group of 5000 workers is exposed to several combinations of concentration and time as follows:

Concentration (mg/m3)	Time (years)
1	25
2	20
3	15
4	10

How many excess cases of cancer are expected to arise from exposure to this airborne carcinogen? (Assume C_i are constant over T_i, N is constant, $I = 20.6$ m^3/day from Table 4.3, and $R = 10^{-9}$ mg^{-1}.)

Solution to Problem 5.3

Use Equation 5.10, since a risk group of constant size is exposed to k combinations of concentration and time:

$$EC = R \cdot I \cdot N \sum_{i=1}^{k} C_i T_i = 10^{-9} \cdot 20.6 \cdot 5000 \sum_{i=1}^{4} C_i T_i$$

$$= 10^{-9} \cdot 20.6 \cdot 5000 \cdot 250(25 + 40 + 45 + 40)$$

$$= 4$$

Problem 5.4

Everyone in a risk group of 1000 workers is exposed to 0.01 mg/m^3 of an airborne carcinogen as follows:

Number	Time (years)
100	5
300	10
400	15
200	20

How many excess cases of cancer are expected? (Assume N_i are constant over T_i, C is constant, $R = 10^{-5}$ mg^{-1}, and $I = 20.6$ m^3/day from Table 4.3.)

Solution to Problem 5.4

Use Equation 5.11, since several risk groups are exposed to the same constant concentration for different times:

$$EC = R \cdot I \cdot C \sum_{i=1}^{k} N_i T_i = 10^{-5} \cdot 20.6 \cdot 0.01 \sum_{i=1}^{4} N_i T_i$$

$$= 10^{-5} \cdot 20.6 \cdot 0.01 \cdot 250(500 + 3000 + 6000 + 4000)$$

$$= 7$$

Problem 5.5

Everyone in a general population risk group of 50,000 people is exposed 8 hours per day for 25 years to an airborne carcinogen as follows:

Number	Concentration (mg/m3)
10,000	0.05
20,000	0.01
10,000	0.005
10,000	0.001

How many excess cases of cancer are expected? (Assume N_i and C_i are constant over 25 years, $R = 10^{-6}$ mg^{-1}, and $I = 9.6$ m3/day from Table 4.3.)

Solution to Problem 5.5

Use Equation 5.12, since several risk groups are exposed to different concentrations for the same period of time:

$$EC = R \cdot I \cdot T \sum_{i=1}^{k} N_i C_i = 10^{-6} \cdot 9.6 \cdot 25 \cdot 365 \sum_{i=1}^{4} N_i C_i$$

$$= 10^{-6} \cdot 9.6 \cdot 25 \cdot 365(500 + 200 + 50 + 10)$$

$$= 67$$

Excess cases due to a latent effect will begin to appear after the minimum latent period has elapsed. The shape of the time distribution of excess cases per year is a complex function primarily of the age distribution of the risk group. Age distribution, in turn, defines the distributions of latent periods. Distributions of latent periods by age are usually unknown for a particular latent effect. Hence, only an average number of excess cases per year can be computed.

The average number of excess cases per year, during the years of their manifestation, can be calculated as follows:

$$EC/year = EC/(E' + T - L') \tag{5.13}$$

where E' = remaining lifetime (in years) of the youngest person in the risk group (see Table 5.2), e.g., $E' = 53$ years at an attained age of 22.

T = years of risk group exposure

L' = minimum human latent period in years

Problem 5.6

What is the average number of excess cases per year for a general population risk group, given: $T = 30$ years, $EC = 94$, $L' = 10$ years, and $E' = 74$ years?

Solution to Problem 5.6

$$EC/year = 94/(74 + 30 - 10) = 1$$

5.3 SENSITIVITY ANALYSIS

The key factor in risk analysis is the risk factor. Those variables which compose the risk factor—experimental response and dose—should be carefully examined for sources of error or uncertainty. This examination may lead to the calculation of several plausible risk factors if any of the following obtain:

- The control group was imperfect. This usually results in an underestimation of the response and excess risk.
- The age distribution of the human or animal study was quite different from that of the human risk group. This could result in an under- or overestimation of response and excess risk due to a difference in competing causes of mortality and/or sensitivity to injury.
- The time of observation from first or last exposure in the human or animal study may have been too short to observe the full impact of all exposure, especially if the response was latent. This would lead to an underestimation of response and excess risk.
- The dose in a human or animal study may have been overestimated due to imperfect knowledge of the minimum concentration and time required to produce a given effect. Ideally, dose should be calculated on the basis of an understanding of the pharmacokinetics of the toxicant. However, complete pharmacokinetic information is rarely available.
- In the computation of dose from a human or animal study, several safety factors may be used. Since the values of these factors are essentially arbitrary, it is likely that there will be several reasonable alternative values of dose.

CHAPTER 6

Acceptable Concentrations

W. H. Hallenbeck

There are several important ideas associated with the calculation and evaluation of an acceptable concentration.

- When an acceptable concentration is based on a human or animal study involving less-than-lifetime exposure and/or observation time, the acceptable concentration should be referred to as provisional.
- NOEL, NOAEL, or LOAEL data from human or animal studies are used in the safety factor method of calculating acceptable concentrations.
- Only LOAEL data from human or animal studies are used in the risk analysis method of calculating acceptable concentrations.
- The safety factor method is used only for those toxicants which are known or assumed to have a nonzero threshold of response.
- The risk analysis method is used only for those toxicants which are known or assumed to have a zero threshold of response (e.g., carcinogens).
- Sometimes a toxicant will produce multiple types of health effects. Whenever both dose-response models (zero and nonzero threshold) apply to a single toxicant, the lowest acceptable concentration (calculated from either the safety factor or risk analysis method) is recommended for adoption.

6.1 RISK ANALYSIS METHOD FOR TOXICANTS WITH ZERO THRESHOLDS (e.g., CARCINOGENS)

Acceptable concentrations can be calculated for a general population or worker risk group on the basis of acceptable individual excess risk or acceptable number of excess cases. There is no national consensus on values for acceptable individual excess risk or an acceptable number of excess cases. As was discussed in more detail in Chapter 1, the FDA and USEPA use an acceptable lifetime individual excess risk of 10^{-6} (one case per million exposed) for general population exposure, and OSHA uses 10^{-3} for worker lifetime exposure (FDA 1985a, 1985b; EPA, 1985; OSHA, 1985). Arguments were presented in Chapter 1 justifying the use of 10^{-5} for worker exposure rather than 10^{-3}.

The procedures for calculating an acceptable concentration are relatively unequivocal for acceptable risks which fall within the range of experimentally observed responses (derived from animal or epidemiology studies). However, acceptable risks such as 10^{-5} and 10^{-6} fall well below the usual experimental response range. For toxicants which are known or assumed to have zero thresholds, linear interpolation is used to calculate the acceptable concentration for acceptable risks between the lowest experimental response and the origin (at zero dose and zero response).

6.1.1 Acceptable Individual Excess Risk

If the acceptable individual excess risk is in the range of experimentally observed responses, Equations 5.1 and 5.2 can be used to calculate the acceptable concentration. The acceptable dose (D_3) is calculated from Equation 5.1 and the acceptable concentration from Equation 5.2.

Usually the acceptable individual excess risk is well below the range of experimentally observed responses. In this case, linear interpolation is recommended between the response observed at the lowest experimental dose and the origin (at zero dose and zero response). The acceptable concentration can be calculated by solving Equation 5.3 for C:

$$C = P/(R \cdot I \cdot T_3) \tag{5.3}$$

Equation 5.3 can be used to calculate acceptable concentrations for air, water, and food, and can be solved for any desired combination of P, I, and T_3 for the general population or workers. The risk factor, R, is obtained from either Equation 5.4 or 5.5. Four special cases of Equation 5.3 are discussed below.

Case 1. Acceptable air concentration for an individual in the general population who is continuously exposed over a lifetime.

$T_3 = (74 - L) \cdot 365$ days, where the human lifetime is 74 years and L is the median human latent period in years for a latent response such as cancer

$I = 20$ m³/day (see Table 4.1)

From Equation 5.3 (let $P = 10^{-6}$):

$$C = P/(R \cdot I \cdot T_3)$$
$$= 10^{-6}/[R \cdot 20 \cdot (74 - L) \cdot 365]$$
$$= 1.4 \cdot 10^{-10}/[R \cdot (74 - L)] \quad \text{mg/m}^3 \quad (6.1)$$

Case 2. Acceptable air concentration for an individual worker who remains at the same job for a working lifetime.

$T_3 = 5$ days/week $\cdot$ 50 weeks/year $\cdot$ (years of exposure adjusted, if necessary, for median latent period and remaining lifetime from last exposure)

$I = 20.6$ m³/day (see Table 4.3)

From Equation 5.3 (let $P = 10^{-5}$):

$$C = P/(R \cdot I \cdot T_3)$$
$$= 10^{-5}/(R \cdot 20.6 \cdot T_3)$$
$$= 4.9 \cdot 10^{-7}/(R \cdot T_3) \quad \text{mg/m}^3 \quad (6.2)$$

Case 3. Acceptable water concentration for an individual in the general population who is exposed daily over a lifetime.

$T_3 = (74 - L) \cdot 365$ days, where the human lifetime is 74 years and L is the median human latent period in years for a latent response such as cancer

$I = 2.5$ ℓ/day (see Table 4.1)

From Equation 5.3 (let $P = 10^{-6}$):

$$C = P/(R \cdot I \cdot T_3)$$
$$= 10^{-6}/[R \cdot 2.5 \cdot (74 - L) \cdot 365]$$
$$= 1.1 \cdot 10^{-9}/[R \cdot (74 - L)] \quad \text{mg/}\ell \quad (6.3)$$

Case 4. Acceptable food concentration for an individual in the general population who is exposed daily over a lifetime.

$T_3 = (74 - L) \cdot 365$ days, where the human lifetime is 74 years and L is the median human latent period in years for a latent response such as cancer

$I = 1.5$ kg/day (see Table 4.1)

From Equation 5.3 (let $P = 10^{-6}$):

$$C = P/(R \cdot I \cdot T_3)$$

$$= 10^{-6}/[R \cdot 1.5 \cdot (74 - L) \cdot 365]$$

$$= 1.8 \cdot 10^{-9}/[R \cdot (74 - L)] \quad \text{mg/kg of food} \quad (6.4)$$

6.1.2   Acceptable Number of Excess Cases

If the acceptable number of excess cases (EC) and size of the risk group (N) are specified, the group excess risk can be calculated from Equation 5.6:

$$EC/N = P = f(D_4) \quad (5.6)$$

If the calculated group excess risk is in the range of experimentally observed responses, Equations 5.6 and 5.7 can be used to calculate the acceptable concentration. The acceptable dose (D_4) is calculated from Equation 5.6 and the acceptable concentration from Equation 5.7.

Usually, the group excess risk is well below the range of experimentally observed responses. In this case, linear interpolation is recommended between the response observed at the lowest experimental dose and the origin (at zero dose and zero response). The acceptable concentration can be calculated by solving Equation 5.11 for C:

$$C = EC/(R \cdot I \cdot \sum_{i=1}^{k} N_i T_i) \quad (5.11)$$

Equation 5.11 can be used to calculate acceptable concentrations for air, water, and food, and can be solved for any desired combination of EC, I, T_i, and N_i for the general population or workers. The risk factor, R, is obtained from either Equation 5.4 or 5.5.

6.2 SAFETY FACTOR METHOD FOR TOXICANTS WITH NONZERO THRESHOLDS

Acceptable concentrations can be calculated for members of a risk group (general population or worker) using the following equation:

$$C = D_j/(I \cdot T) \qquad (6.5)$$

where C = acceptable concentration in mg per unit of contaminated media
 D_j = no-effect dose (in mg) calculated from either Equation 4.4 or 4.5
 I = intake in units of contaminated human media (air, water, or food) per day (see Tables 4.1–4.3)
 T = exposure time (in days)

Concerning D_j, there are two situations when a lowest effective dose should be used in place of a no-effect dose: (a) when a no-effect dose is unavailable and knowledge of the mechanism of toxicity indicates a nonzero threshold dose-response relationship; (b) when a no-effect dose exists but is based on a study with serious weaknesses, e.g., short exposure time, short observation time, inappropriate route of exposure, or small sample size.

Equation 6.5 can be used to calculate acceptable concentrations for air, water, and food, and can be solved for any desired combination of intake and exposure time for the general population or workers.

Case 1. Acceptable air concentration for an individual in the general population who is continuously exposed over a lifetime.

$$T = 74 \cdot 365 = 27010 \text{ days}$$

$$I = 20 \text{ m}^3/\text{day (see Table 4.1)}$$

From Equation 6.5,

$$C = D_j/(I \cdot T)$$

$$= D_j/(20 \cdot 27010)$$

$$= 1.9 \cdot 10^{-6} \cdot D_j \quad \text{mg/m}^3 \qquad (6.6)$$

Case 2. Acceptable air concentration for a worker who remains at the same job for a working lifetime.

$$T = 5 \text{ days/week} \cdot 50 \text{ weeks/year} \cdot 50 \text{ years}$$

$$= 12500 \text{ days}$$

$$I = 20.6 \text{ m}^3/\text{day (see Table 4.3)}$$

From Equation 6.5,

$$C = D_j/(I \cdot T)$$
$$= D_j/(20.6 \cdot 12500)$$
$$= 3.9 \cdot 10^{-6} \cdot D_j \quad mg/m^3 \qquad (6.7)$$

Case 3. Acceptable water concentration for an individual in the general population who is exposed daily over a lifetime.

$$T = 74 \cdot 365 = 27010 \text{ days}$$
$$I = 2.5 \text{ } \ell/\text{day (see Table 4.1)}$$

From Equation 6.5,

$$C = D_j/(I \cdot T)$$
$$= D_j/(2.5 \cdot 27010)$$
$$= 1.5 \cdot 10^{-5} \cdot D_j \quad mg/\ell \qquad (6.8)$$

Case 4. Acceptable food concentration for an individual in the general population who is exposed daily over a lifetime.

$$T = 74 \cdot 365 = 27010 \text{ days}$$
$$I = 1.5 \text{ kg/day (see Table 4.1)}$$

From Equation 6.5,

$$C = D_j/(I \cdot T)$$
$$= D_j/(1.5 \cdot 27010)$$
$$= 2.5 \cdot 10^{-5} \cdot D_j \quad mg/kg \text{ of food} \qquad (6.9)$$

Problem 6.1

Calculate an acceptable air concentration for workers exposed for a working lifetime to a chemical which causes lung damage in rats and is assumed to have a nonzero threshold. Use the following results from a rat study.

Control group
Comparison to historical controls: no evidence of premature deaths
Time of sacrifice: all surviving rats were sacrificed at 18 months
Initial number: 100
Number of rats with lung damage: 0

Test group
Inhalation exposure conditions (highest no-effect): 20 mg/m^3, 6 hours/day
   for a median of 12 months
Time of sacrifice: all surviving rats were sacrificed at 18 months
Comparisons of weight and survival curves: no differences between test
   and control rats
Median adult weight: 0.4 kg
Initial number exposed: 100
Number of rats with lung damage: 0

Solution to Problem 6.1

Calculate the highest no-effect human dose from Equation 4.4:

$$D_1 = \frac{C_1 \cdot I_1}{W_1 \displaystyle\prod_{i=1}^{6} F_i} \cdot 70 \cdot \frac{T_1}{E_1 - L_1} \cdot (74 - L) \cdot 365$$

$$= \frac{20 \cdot 0.061}{0.4 \cdot 1000} \cdot 70 \cdot \frac{1}{2} \cdot 74 \cdot 365$$

$$= 2883 \text{ mg}$$

where D_1 = highest no-effect human dose in mg
        C_1 = 20 mg/m^3
        W_1 = 0.4 kg
        I_1 = $0.105(0.4/0.113)^{2/3} \cdot$ (6 h/d / 24 h/d)
            = 0.061 m^3/day of contaminated air (see footnote g in Table 4.1)

$$\prod_{i=1}^{6} F_i = 1000, \quad \begin{array}{l} F_1 = 10 \\ F_2 = 10 \\ F_3 = F_4 = F_5 = 1 \\ F_6 = 10 \end{array}$$

        T_1 = 1 year
        E_1 = 2 years (see Table 4.1)
        L_1 = L = 0

Calculate the acceptable concentration from Equation 6.7:

$$C = 3.9 \cdot 10^{-6} \cdot D_1$$

$$= 3.9 \cdot 10^{-6} \cdot 2883$$

$$= 0.011 \text{ mg/m}^3$$

Problem 6.2

Calculate an acceptable water concentration for lifetime general population exposure to a chemical which causes liver damage in rats and is assumed to have a nonzero threshold. Use the following results from a rat study.

Control group
Comparison to historical controls: no evidence of premature deaths
Time of sacrifice: all surviving rats were sacrificed at 18 months
Initial number: 100
Number of rats with liver damage: 0

Test group
Ingestion exposure conditions (lowest effective): 20 mg/ℓ, 24 hours/day
for a median of 3 months
Time of sacrifice: all surviving rats were sacrificed at 18 months
Comparisons of weight and survival curves: no differences between test
and control rats
Median adult weight: 0.5 kg
Initial number exposed: 150
Number of rats with liver damage: 25

Solution to Problem 6.2

Calculate the lowest effective human dose from Equation 4.4:

$$D_1 = \frac{C_1 \cdot I_1}{W_1 \prod\limits_{i=1}^{6} F_i} \cdot 70 \cdot \frac{T_1}{E_1 - L_1} \cdot (74 - L) \cdot 365$$

$$= \frac{20 \cdot 0.025}{0.5 \cdot 10^4} \cdot 70 \cdot \frac{0.25}{2} \cdot 74 \cdot 365$$

$$= 23.6 \text{ mg}$$

where D_1 = lowest effective human dose in mg
  C_1 = 20 mg/ℓ
  W_1 = 0.5 kg
  I_1 = 0.025 ℓ/day of contaminated water (see Table 4.1)

$$\prod_{i=1}^{6} F_i = 10000, \quad \begin{aligned} F_1 &= 10 \\ F_2 &= 10 \\ F_3 &= F_4 = 1 \\ F_5 &= 10 \\ F_6 &= 10 \end{aligned}$$

$T_1 = 0.25$ year
$E_1 = 2$ years (see Table 4.1)
$L_1 = L = 0$

Calculate test and control group response from Equations 4.6 and 4.7.

$$\begin{aligned} P_t &= X_t/N_t \\ &= 25/150 \\ &= 0.17 \\ P_c &= X_c/N_c \\ &= 0/100 \\ &= 0 \end{aligned}$$

The difference between P_t and P_c is statistically significant (P-value < 1%; see Table 4.7 for a Poisson variable). P_t and P_c can be treated statistically as Poisson variables, since both sample sizes are greater than 50 and both response frequencies are less than 20%. It is important to confirm whether or not the difference is statistically significant in order to determine if the dose is a no-effect or lowest effective dose. If the difference between P_t and P_c were not statistically significant, the dose would be a no-effect dose and $F_5 = 1$.

The acceptable water concentration can be calculated from Equation 6.8:

$$\begin{aligned} C &= 1.5 \cdot 10^{-5} \cdot D_1 \\ &= 1.5 \cdot 10^{-5} \cdot 23.6 \\ &= 3.5 \cdot 10^{-4} \end{aligned}$$

CHAPTER 7

Example: Environmental and Occupational Exposure to a Hypothetical Industrial Toxicant

W. H. Hallenbeck

Many equations were presented in Chapters 4, 5, and 6. The following is a selected listing of the most important equations which would be used in almost every risk assessment.

Calculation of human dose in mg from an animal or human study (Equation 4.3):

$$D_j = \frac{C_j \cdot I_j}{W_j \prod\limits_{i=1}^{n} F_i} \cdot 70 \cdot \frac{T_j}{E_j - L_j} \cdot (74 - L) \cdot 365$$

Calculation of test and control group response from an animal or human study (Equations 4.6 – 4.9):

$$P_t = X_t/N_t = Obs/N_t$$

$$P_c = X_c/N_c = Exp/N_t$$

Calculation of control-adjusted test group response from an animal or human study (Equations 4.19, 4.21, and 4.24):

$$P_e = (P_t - P_c)/(1 - P_c)$$
$$P'_e = (P'_t - P'_c)/(1 - P'_c)$$
$$P'_e = (P'_t - P_c)/(1 - P_c)$$

Calculation of dose (in mg) for an individual at risk (Equation 5.2):

$$D_3 = C \cdot I \cdot T_3$$

Calculation of individual excess risk, assuming linear interpolation (Equation 5.3):

$$P = R \cdot D_3 = R \cdot C \cdot I \cdot T_3$$

Calculation of risk factors (Equations 5.4 and 5.5):

$$R = P_e/D_j$$
$$R' = P'_e/D_j$$

Calculation of risk group dose in mg (Equation 5.7):

$$D_4 = C \cdot I \cdot T$$

Calculation of excess cases in a risk group, assuming linear interpolation (Equation 5.9):

$$EC = R \cdot I \sum_{i=1}^{k} C_i T_i N_i$$

Calculation of excess cases per year in a risk group (Equation 5.13):

$$EC/year = EC/(E + T - L')$$

Calculation of acceptable concentration based on linear interpolation and acceptable excess risk (Equation 5.3):

$$C = P/(R \cdot I \cdot T_3)$$

Calculation of acceptable concentration based on linear interpolation and acceptable excess cases (Equation 5.11):

$$C = EC/\left(R \cdot I \sum_{i=1}^{k} N_i T_i\right)$$

Calculation of acceptable concentration based on the safety factor method (Equation 6.5):

$$C = D_j/(I \cdot T)$$

The following example demonstrates the calculation of individual excess risk, excess cases, excess cases per year, and acceptable concentrations for general population and worker exposure to a toxicant with a zero threshold.

A source of air emissions is proposed to operate continuously for 65 years. Air modeling data show that 1.11 million people living in the surrounding area will be exposed to airborne concentrations of a contaminant as follows:

Number	Concentration (mg/m^3)
10^4	$3 \cdot 10^{-5}$
10^5	$1 \cdot 10^{-5}$
10^6	$5 \cdot 10^{-6}$
$1.11 \cdot 10^6$	

Also, 200 workers per day will be exposed at $3 \cdot 10^{-4}$ mg/m^3. The contaminant has caused lung cancer in a rat study and an occupational epidemiology study.

Results of the rat study

Control group
Comparison to historical controls: no evidence of premature deaths
Time of sacrifice: all surviving rats were sacrificed at 24 months of age
Initial number: 100
Number surviving at least as long as the minimum latent period: 100
Number of tumor-bearing animals (TBA): 10

Test group
Inhalation exposure conditions (lowest effective): 20 mg/m^3, 5 days/ week, 6 hours/day for a median of 12 months, beginning at 8 weeks of age
Comparison of survival curves: slight evidence of premature deaths compared to controls
Time of sacrifice: all surviving animals were sacrificed at 24 months of age
Comparison of weight curves: no difference from controls
Median adult weight: 0.5 kg
Initial number exposed: 200
Number surviving at least as long as the minimum latent period: 160
Number of tumor-bearing animals (TBA) in the 160 rats at risk: 40
Median latent period: 20 months

Results of the occupational epidemiology study

Inhalation exposure conditions: 5 mg/m^3 (estimated), 50 weeks/year, 5 days/week, 8 hours/day for a median of 10 years per worker
Median time of observation of exposed workers: 15 years after last exposure
Number of workers exposed: 333
Number surviving at least as long as the minimum latent period: 300
Number of cases of lung cancer observed in the 300 workers at risk: 45
Number of cases of lung cancer expected in the 300 workers at risk: 20
Median latent period: 20 years
Minimum latent period: 10 years
Median age at first exposure: 39 years

Calculate the maximum individual excess risk, excess cases, excess cases per year, and acceptable concentrations for the general population and workers given the following assumptions:

• The general population will be continuously exposed for 65 years.
• The number of people in each of the general population exposure subgroups will remain constant for 65 years.
• The exposure concentration for each general population subgroup will remain constant for 65 years.
• Workers will be exposed for 8 hours/day, 5 days/week, 50 weeks/year for 65 years (50 years maximum for an individual worker).
• The size of the worker risk group will remain constant for 65 years.
• All workers will be exposed to one concentration over 65 years.
• The workers will have no off-work exposure to the contaminant.

7.1 SOLUTIONS BASED ON A RAT STUDY

7.1.1 Lowest Effective Human Dose from Equation 4.4

$$D_1 = \frac{C_1 \cdot I_1}{W_1 \prod\limits_{i=1}^{6} F_i} \cdot 70 \cdot \frac{T_1}{E_1 - L_1} \cdot (74 - L) \cdot 365$$

$$= \frac{20 \cdot 0.071}{0.5 \cdot 1000} \cdot 70 \cdot \frac{0.11}{0.33} \cdot (74 - 20) \cdot 365$$

$$= 1.3 \cdot 10^3 \text{ mg}$$

where D_1 = human lowest effective dose in mg
$\quad C_1$ = 20 mg/m^3
$\quad W_1$ = 0.5 kg
$\quad I_1$ = 0.105 (0.5/0.113)$^{2/3}$ · (6 h/d / 24 h/d)
$\quad\quad$ = 0.071 m^3/day of contaminated air (see footnote g in Table 4.1)

$$\prod_{i=1}^{6} F_i = 1000,$$

$\quad F_1$ = 10
$\quad F_2$ = 10
$\quad F_3$ = F_4 = F_5 = 1 (F_4 is used only when calculating acceptable concentrations. Since F_4 = 1, it has no impact in any calculations, and is included here for convenience purposes only.)
$\quad F_6$ = 10

T_1 = 5 d/w · 4 w/m · 2 m / (365 d/y) = 0.11 year, since unadjusted time of exposure was 12 months, median latency was 20 months, remaining lifetime and observation time from last exposure were both 10 months, and exposure began at 2 months of age.
E_1 = 2 years (see Table 4.1)
L_1 = 20/12 = 1.67 years
L = 20 years (from the epidemiology study)

7.1.2 Test and Control Group Response

From Equations 4.6 and 4.7,

$$P_t = X_t/N_t$$

$$= 40/160$$

$$= 0.25$$

$$P_c = X_c/N_c$$
$$= 10/100$$
$$= 0.1$$

where N_t = 160 rats at risk rather than 200 because only 80% of the initial number exposed survived at least as long as the minimum latent period from first exposure

7.1.3   Statistical significance of the difference between the test and control group responses

The normal approximation to the binomial must be used since the test response is greater than 20% (hence, the Poisson approximation cannot be used). From Equation 4.17:

$$z = (P_t - P_c)/\{pq\ [(1/N_t) + (1/N_c)]\}^{1/2}$$

$$= (0.25 - 0.1)/\{0.192 \cdot 0.808\ [(1/160) + (1/100)]\}^{1/2}$$

$$= 2.99\ (\text{P-value} = 0.001,\ \text{see Table 4.6})$$

where $P_t = 0.25$
$P_c = 0.1$
$p = (X_t + X_c)/(N_t + N_c)$
$\quad = (40 + 10)/(160 + 100) = 50/260 = 0.192$
$q = (1 - p) = (1 - 0.192) = 0.808$
$N_t = 160$
$N_c = 100$
$N_t p,\ N_t q,\ N_c p,$ and $N_c q$ are all greater than five

The difference between P_t and P_c is statistically significant.

7.1.4   Control-Adjusted Test Group Response

From Equation 4.19,

$$P_e = (P_t - P_c)/(1 - P_c)$$

$$= (0.25 - 0.1)/(1 - 0.1)$$

$$= 0.17$$

7.1.5   Upper Limit of the Control-Adjusted Test Group Response

From Equation 4.21,

$$P'_e = (P'_t - P'_c)/(1 - P'_c)$$

$$= (0.34 - 0.04)/(1 - 0.04)$$

$$= 0.31$$

where $P'_t(99\%) = 0.34$ can be found in Appendix 1 under $N_t = 160$ and
$\quad X_t = 40$
$P'_c(1\%) = 0.04$ can be found in Appendix 1 under $N_c = 100$ and
$\quad X_c = 10$

Note that P'_e is almost twice P_e (0.31 vs 0.17).

7.1.6 Maximum Dose to an Individual in the General Population

From Equation 5.2,

$$D_3 = C \cdot I \cdot T_3$$

$$= 3 \cdot 10^{-5} \cdot 20 \cdot 19710$$

$$= 12 \text{ mg}$$

where D_3 = maximum dose in mg to an individual in the general population
C = $3 \cdot 10^{-5}$ mg/m^3 (given)
I = 20 m^3/day (see Table 4.1)
T_3 = 19710 days
$\quad$ = $(T - L + E') \cdot 365$
$\quad$ = $(65 - 20 + 9) \cdot 365$

Since 12 mg is well below the lowest effective dose of $1.3 \cdot 10^3$ mg (see Section 7.1.1), linear interpolation must be used to calculate individual excess risk and excess cases.

7.1.7. Maximum Individual Worker Dose

From Equation 5.2,

$$D_3 = C \cdot I \cdot T_3$$

$$= 3 \cdot 10^{-4} \cdot 20.6 \cdot 9750$$

$$= 60 \text{ mg}$$

where D_3 = maximum individual worker dose in mg
C = $3 \cdot 10^{-4}$ mg/m^3 (given)
I = 20.6 m^3/day (see Table 4.3)
T_3 = 9750 days
$\quad$ = 5 d/w $\cdot$ 50 w/y $\cdot$ $(T - L + E')$
$\quad$ = $250(50 - 20 + 9)$. T = 50 years, assuming a working lifetime begins at age 15 and ends at age 65.

Since 60 mg is well below the lowest effective dose of $1.3 \cdot 10^3$ mg (see Section 7.1.1), linear interpolation must be used to calculate individual excess risk and excess cases.

7.1.8 Risk Factors

From Equations 5.4 and 5.5,

$$R = P_e/D_1$$
$$= 0.17/1.3 \cdot 10^3$$
$$= 1.3 \cdot 10^{-4} \text{ mg}^{-1}$$
$$R' = P'_e/D_1$$
$$= 0.31/1.3 \cdot 10^3$$
$$= 2.4 \cdot 10^{-4} \text{ mg}^{-1}$$

7.1.9 Maximum Individual Excess Risk for the General Population and Workers

From Equation 5.3,

$$P = R' \cdot D_3$$
$$= 2.4 \cdot 10^{-4} \cdot 12 = 2.9 \cdot 10^{-3} \text{ (general population)}$$
$$= 2.4 \cdot 10^{-4} \cdot 60 = 0.014 \text{ (workers)}$$

The calculated risks are well below those tabulated for the risk of developing lung cancer in the U.S. general population (see Table 4.4). Hence, the calculated risks are plausible.

7.1.10 Excess Cases and Excess Cases per Year for the General Population

Since several risk groups are exposed to different concentrations for the same period of time, Equation 5.12 is used to calculate the number of excess cases:

$$EC = R' \cdot I \cdot T \sum_{i=1}^{k} N_i C_i$$

$$= 2.4 \cdot 10^{-4} \cdot 20 \cdot 23725 \sum_{i=1}^{3} N_i C_i$$

$$= 114[(10^4 \cdot 3 \cdot 10^{-5}) + (10^5 \cdot 10^{-5}) + (10^6 \cdot 5 \cdot 10^{-6})]$$

$$= 718$$

where EC = excess cases in the general population
 R' = $2.4 \cdot 10^{-4}$ mg^{-1}
 I = 20 m^3 day (see Table 4.1)
 T = 65 years $\cdot$ 365 days/year
  = 23725 days of risk group exposure

$$\sum_{i=1}^{3} N_i \, C_i = 6.3$$

From Equation 5.13,

$$
\begin{aligned}
\text{EC/year} &= \text{EC}/(\text{E}' + \text{T} - \text{L}') \\
&= 718/(74 + 65 - 10) \\
&= 6
\end{aligned}
$$

where EC = 718
 E' = 74 years = human lifetime = remaining lifetime of the youngest person in the risk group
 T = 65 years of risk group exposure
 L' = 10 years (minimum latent period)

Thus, 10 years after initial exposure, excess cases will begin to appear in the general population and continue for the next 129 years at an average rate of 6 excess cases of lung cancer per year.

7.1.11 Excess Cases and Excess Cases per Year for Workers

Since the worker risk group is of constant size and will be exposed to one concentration for 65 years, use Equation 5.8 to calculate the number of excess cases:

$$
\begin{aligned}
\text{EC} &= \text{R}' \cdot \text{C} \cdot \text{I} \cdot \text{T} \cdot \text{N} \\
&= 2.4 \cdot 10^{-4} \cdot 3 \cdot 10^{-4} \cdot 20.6 \cdot 16250 \cdot 200 \\
&= 5
\end{aligned}
$$

where EC = excess cases in the worker risk group
 R' = $2.4 \cdot 10^{-4}$ mg^{-1}
 I = 20.6 m^3/day (see Table 4.3)
 T = 5 days/week $\cdot$ 50 weeks/year $\cdot$ 65 years
  = 16250 days of risk group exposure
 N = 200 workers
 C = $3 \cdot 10^{-4}$ mg/m^3 (given)

From Equation 5.13,

$$EC/year = EC/(E' + T - L')$$
$$= 5/(60 + 65 - 10)$$
$$= 0.04$$

where EC = 5

E' = 60 years = remaining lifetime (see Table 5.2) of the youngest
worker in the risk group (assume an age of 15 years)

T = 65 years of risk group exposure

L' = 10 years (minimum latent period)

Thus, 10 years after initial exposure, excess cases will begin to appear in the worker risk group and continue for the next 115 years at average rate of 0.04 cases of lung cancer per year.

7.1.12 Acceptable Concentrations for the General Population

Acceptable concentrations can be based on either acceptable individual excess risk or an acceptable number of excess cases. Let the acceptable individual excess risk equal 10^{-6}. Since $P = 10^{-6}$ is much less than the lowest experimental response of 0.17 (see Section 7.1.4), linear interpolation should be used to calculate the acceptable concentration. From Equation 5.3,

$$C = P/(R' \cdot I \cdot T_3)$$
$$= 10^{-6}/(2.4 \cdot 10^{-4} \cdot 20 \cdot 19710)$$
$$= 1.1 \cdot 10^{-8} \text{ mg/m}^3$$

where C = acceptable concentration in mg/m^3

P = 10^{-6} = acceptable individual excess risk

R' = $2.4 \cdot 10^{-4} \text{ mg}^{-1}$

I = 20 m^3/day (see Table 4.1)

T_3 = 19710 days (see Section 7.1.6)

Note that the acceptable concentration (based on $P = 10^{-6}$) is several orders of magnitude less than the projected exposure concentrations of $3 \cdot 10^{-5}$, 10^{-5}, and $5 \cdot 10^{-6}$ mg/m^3.

Let the acceptable number of excess cases equal one. From Equation 5.6,

$$P = EC/N$$
$$= 1/(1.11 \cdot 10^6)$$
$$= 9 \cdot 10^{-7}$$

Since $P = 9 \cdot 10^{-7}$ is much less than the lowest experimental response of 0.17 (see Section 7.1.4), linear interpolation must be used to calculate the acceptable concentration. From Equation 5.8,

$$C = EC/(R' \cdot I \cdot T \cdot N)$$

$$= 1/(2.4 \cdot 10^{-4} \cdot 20 \cdot 23725 \cdot 1.11 \cdot 10^6)$$

$$= 7.9 \cdot 10^{-9} \text{ mg/m}^3$$

where C = acceptable concentration in mg/m^3
EC = 1 = acceptable number of excess cases
R' = $2.4 \cdot 10^{-4}$ mg^{-1}
I = 20 m^3/day (see Table 4.1)
T = 23725 days (see Section 7.1.10)
N = $1.11 \cdot 10^6$ (given)

Note that the acceptable concentration (based on $EC = 1$) is several orders of magnitude less than the projected exposure concentrations of $3 \cdot 10^{-5}$, 10^{-5}, and $5 \cdot 10^{-6}$ mg/m^3.

7.1.13 Acceptable Concentrations for Workers

Acceptable concentrations can be based on either acceptable individual excess risk or an acceptable number of excess cases. Let the acceptable individual excess risk equal 10^{-5}. Since $P = 10^{-5}$ is much less than the lowest experimental response of 0.17 (see Section 7.1.4), linear interpolation should be used to calculate the acceptable concentration. From Equation 5.3,

$$C = P/(R' \cdot I \cdot T_3)$$

$$= 10^{-5}/(2.4 \cdot 10^{-4} \cdot 20.6 \cdot 9750)$$

$$= 2.1 \cdot 10^{-7} \text{ mg/m}^3$$

where C = acceptable concentration in mg/m^3
P = 10^{-5} = acceptable individual excess risk
R' = $2.4 \cdot 10^{-4}$ mg^{-1}
I = 20.6 m^3/day (see Table 4.3)
T_3 = 9750 days (see Section 7.1.7)

Note that the acceptable concentration (based on $P = 10^{-5}$) is several orders of magnitude less than the projected exposure concentration of $3 \cdot 10^{-4}$ mg/m^3.

Let the acceptable number of excess cases equal one. From Equation 5.6,

$$P = EC/N$$

$$= 1/200$$

$$= 5 \cdot 10^{-3}$$

Since $P = 5 \cdot 10^{-3}$ is much less than the lowest experimental response of 0.17 (see Section 7.1.4), linear interpolation must be used to calculate the acceptable concentration. From Equation 5.8,

$$C = EC/(R' \cdot I \cdot T \cdot N)$$

$$= 1/(2.4 \cdot 10^{-4} \cdot 20.6 \cdot 16250 \cdot 200)$$

$$= 6.2 \cdot 10^{-5} \text{ mg/m}^3$$

where C = acceptable concentration in mg/m^3
EC = 1 = acceptable number of excess cases
R' = $2.4 \cdot 10^{-4}$ mg^{-1}
I = 20.6 m^3/day (see Table 4.3)
N = 200 (given)
T = 16250 days (see Section 7.1.11)

Note that the acceptable concentration (based on $EC = 1$) is about 20% of the projected exposure concentration of $3 \cdot 10^{-4}$ mg/m^3.

7.2   SOLUTIONS BASED ON AN OCCUPATIONAL EPIDEMIOLOGY STUDY

7.2.1   Lowest Effective Human Dose

From Equation 4.5,

$$D_2 = \frac{C_2 \cdot I_2}{\displaystyle\prod_{i=1}^{5} F_i} \cdot T_2 \cdot 365$$

$$= \frac{5 \cdot 20.6}{100} \cdot 3.4 \cdot 365$$

$$= 1.3 \cdot 10^3 \text{ mg}$$

where D_2 = lowest effective human dose in mg
C_2 = 5 mg/m^3 (given)
I_2 = 20.6 m^3/day (see Table 4.3)

$$\prod_{i=1}^{5} F_i = 100, \quad \begin{aligned} F_1 &= 10 \\ F_2 &= 10 \end{aligned}$$

$F_3 = F_4 = F_5 = F_6 = 1$ (F_4 is used only when calculating acceptable concentrations. Since $F_4 = 1$, it has no impact in any calculations and is included here for convenience purposes only.)

$T_2 = 5$ y $\cdot$ 50 w/y $\cdot$ 5 d/w / (365 d/y) = 3.4 years since unadjusted median exposure time was 10 years, median latency was 20 years, median time of observation from last exposure was 15 years, remaining lifetime from last exposure was (74 – 49) = 25 years, and median age at first exposure was 39 years.

7.2.2 Test and Control Group Response

From Equations 4.8 and 4.9,

$$P_t = Obs/N_t$$

$$= 45/300$$

$$= 0.15$$

$$P_c = Exp/N_t$$

$$= 20/300$$

$$= 0.067$$

where N_t = 300 workers at risk rather than 333 because only 90% of those exposed survived at least as long as the minimum latent period from first exposure.

7.2.3 Statistical Significance of the Difference Between the Test and Control Group Responses

The Poisson approximation to the binomial can be used since both responses are less than 20% and both sample sizes are greater than 50. Enter Table 4.7 at 20 responses: 45 is greater than 33.1. Hence, the difference between observed and expected responses is statistically significant, with a P-value of less than 1%.

7.2.4   Control-Adjusted Test Group Response

From Equation 4.19,

$$P_e = (P_t - P_c)/(1 - P_c)$$
$$= (0.15 - 0.067)/(1 - 0.067)$$
$$= 0.089$$

7.2.5   Upper Limit of the Control-Adjusted Test Group Response

From Equation 4.24,

$$P'_e = (P'_t - P_c)/(1 - P_c)$$
$$= (0.211 - 0.067)/(1 - 0.067)$$
$$= 0.15$$

where $P'_t(99\%) = 63.23/300$ (see Table 4.7)
$$= 0.211$$

7.2.6   Maximum Dose to an Individual in the General Population

$$D_3 = 12 \text{ mg (see Section 7.1.6)}$$

7.2.7   Maximum Individual Worker Dose

$$D_3 = 60 \text{ mg (see Section 7.1.7)}$$

7.2.8   Risk Factors

From Equations 5.4 and 5.5,

$$R = P_e/D_2$$
$$= 0.089/1.3 \cdot 10^3 \text{ mg}$$
$$= 6.8 \cdot 10^{-5} \text{ mg}^{-1}$$

$$R' = P'_e/D_2$$
$$= 0.15/1.3 \cdot 10^3 \text{ mg}$$
$$= 1.2 \cdot 10^{-4} \text{ mg}^{-1}$$

The remainder of the solutions for Section 7.2 are identical in form to Sections 7.1.9 – 7.1.13.

CHAPTER 8

Example: Environmental Exposure to a Natural Toxicant, Radon-222 and Its Daughters

K. M. Cunningham and W. H. Hallenbeck

This chapter contains a detailed example of the use of the methodology set out in Chapters 2 through 6. A risk assessment is carried out to determine the lung cancer risks to the general population due to exposure to commonly encountered levels of the radioisotope radon-222 and its short-lived radioactive daughters. The objectives of this risk assessment are:

1. To estimate lung cancer risks to the general population due to inhalation of average, moderately high, and high indoor radon and radon daughter levels.
2. To recommend an acceptable concentration which would yield a lung cancer risk to the general population of less than one per 100,000.

To attain these objectives a risk assessment was conducted which illustrates the following:

- exposure characterization
- evaluation of the qualitative and quantitative aspects of epidemiological data

- use of more than one epidemiological study for development of risk equations
- adjustments for latency which vary with each epidemiological study
- risk factor analysis
- analysis of risk in the experimental and subexperimental dose ranges
- use of one type of radiological data
- sensitivity analysis based upon varying exposure parameters
- calculation of an acceptable exposure based upon acceptable individual risk
- evaluation of results in the context of other risk analyses and current regulatory activities

Depending on the type and availability of data for a risk assessment, an analysis of exposure, dose, and response characteristics may be more or less complex than what is described in this chapter. Radon exposure is a relatively well investigated health problem in comparison to most environmental and occupational exposures; consequently, there was a large data base available for the analysis of this toxicant.

8.1 EXPOSURE CHARACTERIZATION

The scenario of exposure considered in this risk assessment is the lifetime exposure via inhalation of radon and its daughters in all indoor environments at levels which are typically found in the United States (nuclear industry related exposures are excluded). This includes airborne exposures in any public, commercial, or residential structure. It has been assumed that the indoor concentration of radon that an individual is exposed to remains relatively constant over the individual's lifetime. However, the methodology presented in this example can be used to calculate risk for a wide range of exposure scenarios.

Radon is a naturally occurring gaseous radioisotope in the uranium-238 decay series. Appendix 5 contains tables of the physical and radiological properties of radon and its short-lived daughters. It emanates from rock, soil, and water containing its parent isotopes. Indoor radon arises from a variety of sources. It is emitted from granite or other uranium-238-containing high-grade metamorphic bedrock. When the rock is overlaid with porous soil, radon gas migrates to the surface. In the United States, soil emissions entering through openings in basements or unpaved floors are major sources of indoor radon (Rundo et al., 1979). The incorporation of radon's parent radioisotopes, primarily radium-226, into building materials results in gradual emission of radon from cinder blocks, bricks, gypsum, gravel, and cement (UNSCEAR,

1982). Water containing radon can also generate significant ambient concentrations in areas where radon in water exceeds 1000 pCi/ℓ (Partridge et al., 1979).

Where radon is present, its daughters will also be found. The short-lived daughters (up to lead-210) occur in rapid succession due to their half-lives, which range from 1.6 x 10^{-4} seconds to 26.8 minutes (see Appendix 5). These include polonium-218, 214, lead-214, and bismuth-214 which produce alpha, beta, and gamma emissions. Other isotopes in the decay scheme occur at very low frequencies (e.g., astatine-218 occurs once in every 5000 radon decays) and are not considered in this example.

Indoor radon and radon daughter concentrations are usually higher than those measured outdoors (George, 1982; Pritchard et al., 1982). Daughters can quickly build up (in less than one hour) in enclosed environments such as homes, offices, and other buildings due to the rapid decay of radon and its daughters (Steinhausler, 1975). This is especially problematic in poorly ventilated areas. Energy saving measures which reduce ventilation rates are expected to increase indoor exposure levels significantly (George, 1982).

Wide variability in indoor radon concentrations exists within small geographic areas, primarily due to differences in the radon entry sites and the ventilation of buildings. While higher radon concentrations have been measured in cellars, a common entry point for radon, negligible time is spent there by most people (George and Breslin, 1980). Consequently, they are not a major exposure site. The radon concentrations in this example are typically found above grade, where the majority of human exposure can be expected to occur.

Many offices and work environments have elevated radon levels (UNSCEAR, 1977). Consequently, all time spent indoors, rather than only the time spent at home, could result in radon exposure.

An extensive review of age, sex, season, and occupation-specific indoor occupancy was conducted recently in England which found an overall average percentage of time spent indoors of 90% (Brown et al., 1981, 1983). Although variations existed among groups in the site of indoor activities – home, work, school – the time spent was relatively constant over all age and sex groups. The average of the two seasonal extremes, winter and summer, is reflected in the 90% value. The results were assumed in this analysis to be similar to U.S. indoor occupancy, due to the similarity between the two countries in work and cultural patterns. A 90% time indoor exposure (7884 hours per year) and a 75-year lifetime are assumed for this risk assessment.

A unique measure, working level months (WLM), which incorporates concentration and time, was used in this example because all available epidemiological studies used WLM instead of measurements of individual radioisotopes. (See Appendix 6 for definitions of radiological units used in this example.) Table 8.1 contains the yearly and lifetime WLMs evaluated for risk in this example. An extensive review of radon levels in the United States was conducted to obtain the radon and WLM values used in this example (Alter, 1984; Rundo and co-workers, 1979, 1981, 1984; Hess et al., 1982; George and Breslin, 1980; Fleischer et al., 1981; George, 1982). The selected WLM values correspond to specific radon levels and are based on assumptions regarding the equilibrium between radon and its daughters which are discussed in Appendix 7. The four exposure levels represent an average, a moderately high, and two high exposure levels found in indoor air. The exposure level of 9 WLM is of most concern to the general population, because it is based upon a radon concentration considered to be the global indoor average, 0.5 picocuries per liter of air (pCi/ℓ) (UNSCEAR, 1982).

Table 8.1.   Exposure of the General Population

Exposure Level	Yearly WLM	Lifetime WLM	Radon Concentration[a] (pCi/ℓ)
Average	0.116	9	0.5
Moderately high	1.16	87	5.0
High	11.60	870	50.0
High	23.20	1739	100.0

[a]A radon daughter ratio of 1/0.6/0.4 and an equilibrium factor of 0.5 are assumed. For an explanation of these two terms and the method of calculating WLM for these assumed values, see Appendix 7. (A thorough understanding of daughter ratio, equilibrium factor, and the method of calculating WLM is not necessary for the comprehension of the major objectives of Chapter 8).

8.2 EVALUATION OF STUDIES

Numerous epidemiological studies of lung cancer have been conducted on populations exposed to radon and its daughters in mines (Wagoner et al., 1965; Archer and Lundin, 1967; Lundin et al., 1971; Snihs, 1973; Sevc et al., 1976; Axelson and Sundell, 1978; Kunz et al., 1979; Fox et al., 1981; Gottleib and Husen, 1982; Edling and Axelson, 1983; Whittemore and McMillan, 1983; Radford and St. Clair Renard, 1984a, 1984b; Samet et al., 1984). Consequently, it was not necessary to utilize animal studies as the basis for this risk assessment. Although there are a large number of epidemiological studies of lung cancer in radon-exposed worker populations, there are a limited number which can be relied upon to estimate risk.

The criteria discussed in Chapters 3 and 4 were utilized to evaluate the epidemiological studies. Many studies were eliminated due to their exposure quantification methods. In some cases, radioisotope concentrations were very crudely estimated, or exposure was not quantified. These studies could not be used for a quantitative risk evaluation. The control groups used in most epidemiological studies were general populations in the same geographic area. This was of concern because of the healthy worker effect discussed in Chapter 3. However, this could not be eliminated as a source of error, due to the unavailability of studies with more accurately matched controls.

Some case control studies were not used in the risk assessment because the studies utilized individuals with non-lung cancers as controls. Since there is good evidence that exposure to radon may cause non-respiratory cancers (Radford and St. Clair Renard, 1984a; Bean, 1982), the use of these individuals as controls could increase the proportion of controls that were actually exposed. As discussed in Chapter 3, basic epidemiological principals indicate that if the disease used as the basis for selection of the controls is affected by the factor being considered (radon exposure), the true association between exposure and the effect can be masked, or an association found which is spurious (Mausner and Bahn, 1974). In this risk assessment, radon exposure may increase various types of cancer; therefore, controls chosen from a cancer registry may have a disproportionately high probability of including exposed individuals. An increase in exposed controls would result in a decrease in the estimate of relative risk attributed to the exposure.

Studies were also eliminated if their results were confounded by smoking. In some cases, smoking histories were not obtained. This is unacceptable in a study evaluating lung cancer risks. The presence of other carcinogens in the environment was not considered in most studies.

Three epidemiological studies of miners were used to assess lung cancer risks. The wide range of risk group exposures evaluated in this risk assessment, 9 to 1739 WLM, were not covered in any single epidemiological study. The epidemiological group, methodology, and results of each study are discussed below. Study characteristics which affect its suitability for risk assessment applications are noted. The number of observed responses were significantly different than expected responses based upon the Poisson and normal tests of statistical significance discussed in Chapter 4.

8.2.1   Swedish Iron Miners Study

This study covers the average exposure range of the general population and is a historical prospective analysis of cancer incidence among Swedish iron miners (Radford and St. Clair Renard, 1984a). It was well designed and meets most criteria discussed in Chapters 3 and 4.

The epidemiological study group consisted of 1,415 men born between 1880 and 1919 who were employed for more than one year underground in Swedish mines between 1897 and 1976. Work records on each miner, available since 1900, were obtained from both company and union records. Vital status, occupation, and cause of death (for all but seven miners) were obtained from parish records, the primary source of vital statistics data in Sweden. Causes of death were confirmed in 70% of respiratory cancers by autopsy. Exposure was well quantified, with an estimated error of ± 30 %.

The first 10 years were subtracted from exposure of each miner to account for a latent period. In addition, the last 5 years of exposure were excluded if they directly preceded death. This yielded a 15-year latency adjustment overall. This minimal latent period is in keeping with the minimal latent periods reported in other studies (Geddes, 1979; Edling and Axelson 1983; Whittemore and McMillan, 1983; Samet et al., 1984).

Smoking histories were obtained for all miners with lung cancer. An analysis of the environment was conducted for other lung carcinogens, including arsenic, chromium, and nickel (these three are suspected respiratory carcinogens). These were not present. Diesel exhaust was not a contributing factor because diesel-powered equipment was not introduced until the 1960's, when 70% of the lung cancer cases had left mining. Iron oxide dust, which was present throughout the mine, has not been shown to cause lung cancer in humans or animals (ACGIH, 1980).

Expected (control) lung cancer rates were obtained from the Swedish Central Statistical Bureau based on national averages which were age, sex, and year specific to the lung cancer cases among the miners. The author also noted that non-miners in the area appeared to have a lower lung cancer rate than the national average; however, there were not sufficient numbers to use their rate in the calculation of the expected number of cases. The use of lung cancer rates among the national population as controls, rather than the local lung cancer rates, could result in an underestimate of effect because the expected cases would be higher than was appropriate for the exposed miners.

Table 8.2 contains a summary of the data from the Swedish study and other studies discussed in subsequent sections.

Table 8.2. Epidemiological Study Data

Cumulative Mean WLM	Observed[a]	Expected	Observed/ Expected
Swedish Iron Miners[b]			
26.8	8	3.4	2.35
73.0	14	3.6	3.89
171.9	18	2.4	7.50
217.7	6	1.0	6.00
Czechoslovakian Uranium Miners[c]			
343	102.3	17.4	5.88
488	117.9	16.5	7.15
716	138.9	17.2	8.08
Colorado Plateau Uranium Miners[d]			
1320	40	5.38	7.43
2760	49	4.56	10.75

[a]Significantly different than expected (P-value < 0.05).
[b]Radford and St. Clair Renard, 1984a.
[c]Sevc et al., 1976.
[d]BEIR, 1980.

8.2.2 Czechoslovakian Uranium Miners Study

The study covering the dose range 343 to 716 WLMs was conducted in Czechoslovakia on uranium miners (Sevc et al., 1976). Exposure levels were estimated based on work histories and extensive measurements of radon levels in the mines. The cumulative WLM exposure estimates are accurate within 30%, according to the authors.

The expected lung cancer rates were obtained from the national average lung cancer mortality rates, specific to the age and birth year of the cases, for Czechoslovakian men. Lung cancer cases among miners were identified through the medical services records, the uranium industry health services, and a national oncological registry.

The smoking rate among cancer cases was *assumed* by Sevc et al. (1976) to be the same as that found in a random sample of other miners (70%), and the minimum followup time in the Czechoslovakian study was 16 years. This is an inadequate followup period, because the average time from initial exposure to death in the Swedish study was 41.3 years for nonsmoking lung cancer cases and 38.8 years for smokers (Radford and St. Clair Renard, 1984a). The Swedish study results suggest a followup period of forty to fifty years after initial exposure would be required to identify all radon-related lung cancers. Consequently, the followup period of the Czechoslovakian study probably resulted in an underestimate of lung cancer cases, because many cases would not yet have been detected. Also, there was no adjustment made to exposure by the study authors for the latent period. These problems would result in an overestimate of exposure and an underestimate of response.

Data from the Czechoslovakian study for the range of 343 to 716 cumulative WLMs are shown in Table 8.2. The Czechoslovakian study provided data on exposures lower than 343 WLM. However, due to the longer followup period and better quality of information provided on exposure and worker characteristics in the Swedish study, the Swedish data were used to cover exposures below 343 WLM.

8.2.3   Colorado Uranium Miners Study

The upper exposure range (1320 to 2760 cumulative WLM) is covered by a study of uranium miners of the Colorado Plateau. The minimum followup period was 11 years. The short followup period in this study led the study authors to conclude that excess cases might increase rapidly at some later date in the nonsmoking group because nonsmokers have relatively longer latency periods (BEIR, 1980). Latency was accounted for by excluding lung cancer deaths and person years occurring in the first ten years after a miner's initial exposure. Expected lung cancer rates were based on age- and year-specific lung cancer death rates for the white male population in Colorado, Utah, New Mexico, and Arizona. To take into account those lung cancer cases diagnosed among living uranium miners, the expected lung cancer rates were adjusted upward by 10%. Detailed smoking data were not available.

Working level measurements in Colorado were averaged for each mine for each year of exposure. Researchers involved in the study, as well as independent reviewers, have determined that the exposure levels were probably overestimated (Lundin et al., 1971; Thomas and McNeill, 1982). The Czechoslovakian data were used preferentially in areas where data from the Colorado and Czechoslovakian studies overlapped (i.e., the lower exposure range of the Colorado data) due to the followup and exposure quantification problems with the Colorado study. Selected data from this study used in the lung cancer risk assessment are shown in Table 8.2.

8.2.4   Epidemiological Study Analysis

RRC and P_e were calculated as follows:

$$RRC = [(Obs/Exp) - 1] / E$$
$$= (P_t - P_c)/(P_c \cdot E) = P_e/(P_c \cdot E)$$
$$P_e = RRC \cdot E \cdot P_c = P_t - P_c$$

where RRC = relative risk coefficient
    Obs = number of cases observed in the experimental group
    Exp = expected number of cases in the experimental group
    P_t = proportion responding adversely in the experimental group
    P_c = proportion expected to respond adversely in the experimental group
    E = exposure in WLMs
    P_e = control-adjusted experimental response = excess risk
        = $(P_t - P_c)$ from Equation 4.18
        = $RRC \cdot E \cdot P_c$

The results are shown in Table 8.3. Data from Table 8.3 were plotted in Figure 8.1, which shows the relative risk coefficient (RRC) and probability (P_e) vs exposure curves over the cumulative exposure range of the three epidemiological studies, 26.8 to 2760 WLMs. Figure 8.1a (RRC vs exposure) shows that the risk per unit of exposure (risk factor) decreases as cumulative exposure increases. Convex upward curves have also been noted for carcinogenic effects in neutron-exposed rats and atomic bomb survivors in Japan (Rossi and Kellerer, 1972; Baum, 1973).

The risk factors, given in terms of the RRC, are lower for the Czechoslovakian and Colorado studies than for the Swedish study. Whether these are the true risk factors based on the trend of decline in RRC as

Table 8.3. Relative Risk Coefficient and Probability Data from Epidemiological Studies

Exposure (WLM)	Relative Risk Coefficient (RRC)[a]	Probability (P_e)[b]
Swedish Iron Miners[c]		
26.8	0.051	0.024
73	0.040	0.051
171.9	0.038	0.113
217.7	0.023	0.087
Czechoslovakian Uranium Miners[d]		
343	0.014	0.083
488	0.013	0.110
716	0.010	0.124
Colorado Uranium Miners[e]		
1320	0.005	0.115
2760	0.004	0.192

[a]Relative risk coefficient = [(observed/expected) – 1]/exposure.
[b]Probability = relative risk coefficient x exposure x background lung cancer risk (0.01736).
[c]Radford and St. Clair Renard, 1984a.
[d]Sevc et al., 1976.
[e]BEIR, 1980.

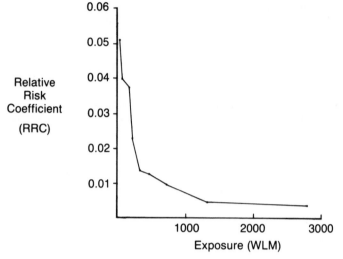

8.1a. Relative Risk Coefficient versus Exposure

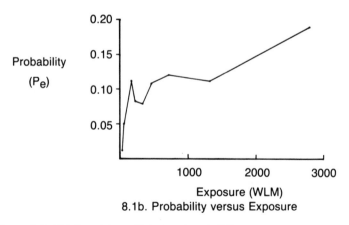

8.1b. Probability versus Exposure

Figure 8.1. Relative risk coefficient and probability versus exposure curves. Based upon epidemiological data in Table 8.3.

exposure increases, or are lower than the actual risk factors due to exposure overestimates, inadequate followup, or other factors, cannot be determined at this time.

8.3 RISK ANALYSIS

8.3.1 Equations for Probability

Equations were developed to describe the individual lifetime probability (P) of dying from lung cancer from the data in Table 8.3. The data were analyzed using various linear and nonlinear regressions to obtain equations which would best fit the data, as determined by a high r^2 (square of the correlation coefficient). The equations, the corresponding ranges they cover, and their r^2 values are shown in Table 8.4.

For population exposures below 26.8 WLM it was necessary to extrapolate outside the observed epidemiological data. A linear extrapolation from 26.8 to 0 WLM was used (similar to Equation 5.3):

$$P = R \cdot E$$
$$= (0.0237/26.8) \cdot E$$
$$= 8.84 \cdot 10^{-4} \cdot E$$

The justification for using the linear extrapolation method was discussed in Chapter 1. The value of using extrapolation from the lowest data point can be demonstrated by reviewing the epidemiological data on radon-induced lung cancer. A comparison of extrapolated results from any of the higher exposure points to a level where the risk *is* known (that is, a comparison *within* the experimental exposure-response range, 26.8 to 2760 WLMs) demonstrates that the lowest data point would lead to the most accurate prediction of response. Since this is known to be true within the experimental range, it is likely to be true in the subexperimental range (less than 26.8 WLMs). This observation supports the use of the lowest known data point at 26.8 WLM for extrapolation into the subexperimental exposure range.

The use of a linear equation for extrapolating risks due to radon and radon daughter exposure is also supported by numerous researchers in

Table 8.4. Equations Relating Probability of Lung Cancer and Exposure[a]

Exposure Range (cumulative working level months)	Risk Equations	r^2
I. 0–26.8	$P = 8.84 \times 10^{-4}$ (E)	none[b]
II. 26.8–171.9	$P = 1.52 \times 10^{-3}$ (E)$^{0.831}$	0.996
III. 171.9–2760	$P = 3.56 \times 10^{-5}$ (E) + 0.0871	0.83

[a]Equations derived from data shown in Table 8.3.
[b]The equation describes the line between the two points (0,0) and (26.8, 0.0237). Therefore, there is no r^2.

the field of radiation epidemiology (Sevc et al., 1976; UNSCEAR, 1977; BEIR, 1980; Radford and St. Clair Renard, 1984a). However, some researchers have suggested that risks based upon a linear extrapolation may be underestimated for high linear energy transfer (LET) emissions, which include radon and its alpha emitting daughters (BEIR, 1980). High LET radiation has been associated with an increasing carcinogenic risk per unit of exposure with decreasing exposure in humans and animals.

8.3.2 Adjustments for Latency

The minimum latency for lung cancer following radon and radon daughter exposure is approximately 15 years (Geddes, 1979; Edling and Axelson, 1983; Whittemore and McMillan, 1983; Samet et al., 1984). The risk group exposures were adjusted for latency in the following manner. A 15-year modification was made to each value from Table 8.1 in the exposure range covered by the Swedish data, 280.4 WLMs or less. This corresponds to the minimum latent period and to the 15-year adjustment made by Radford and St. Clair Renard (1984a) to the exposure of each miner in the Swedish study. The modified population exposure values are shown in Table 8.5. An example of the adjustment for the 9 WLM exposure level shown in Table 8.1 follows:

$$75 \text{ years} - 15 \text{ years latency adjustment}$$

$$= 60 \text{ years of effective exposure}$$

$$\frac{60 \text{ years effective exposure}}{75 \text{ years lifetime exposure}} = 0.8$$

$$0.8 \times 9 \text{ WLMs exposure} = 7 \text{ WLMs exposure}$$

The Czechoslovakian study group's exposure was not adjusted for latency by the study authors (Sevc et al., 1976; Kunz et al., 1978, 1979). Consequently, the risk group exposures were not modified in this example for exposures in the range of the Czechoslovakian data, 280.4 to 1018.0 WLMs. Colorado data were adjusted by the study authors for 10

Table 8.5. General Population Exposure Adjusted for Latency

Cumulative WLM[a]	Cumulative WLM Adjusted for Latency
9	7
87	70
870	870
1739	1507

[a]Taken from Table 8.1

years of latency. Therefore, 10 years of exposure were subtracted from the risk group exposures covered by that study, i.e., those greater than 1018 WLMs. The adjustment was made in the manner shown above. The exposure levels from Table 8.1, adjusted for latency (unadjusted in the Czechoslovakian range), are shown in Table 8.5. The exposure intervals between the three epidemiological data sets were divided in half and assigned to the nearest data set. The cumulative exposure values in Table 8.5 were used in probability calculations to determine risk levels for the risk group. Note that the latency adjustments could not be made until the epidemiological studies had been selected in order to match the adjustments of the experimental group and the risk group.

8.3.3   Calculations of Risks

Using equations for the lifetime probabilities of lung cancer mortality from Table 8.4, the individual probabilities of dying of lung cancer were calculated for risk group exposure levels in Table 8.5. These probabilities are given in Table 8.6. The final column, the risk per 100,000 exposed people, was obtained by multiplying individual probabilities in column 2 by 100,000. The range of risks shown in Table 8.6 is 6.2 per thousand to 140 per thousand.

Table 8.6.   Lifetime Probability of Lung Cancer in the General Population Due to Radon and Radon Daughter Exposure

Exposure in Working Level Months[a]	Individual Probability of Lung Cancer[b]	Risk per 100,000 Population[c]
7	$6.2 \cdot 10^{-3}$ (I)	620
70	$5.2 \cdot 10^{-2}$ (II)	5,200
870	$1.2 \cdot 10^{-1}$ (III)	12,000
1507	$1.4 \cdot 10^{-1}$ (III)	14,000

[a]Values taken from Table 8.5.
[b]Calculated from equations in Table 8.4. Equation numbers shown in parentheses.
[c]Calculated by multiplying values in column 2 by 100,000.

8.3.4   Sensitivity Analysis

A sensitivity analysis was carried out to determine the effect on risk of varying the assumption that all time spent indoors resulted in exposure. In some cases exposure may occur *only* in the home or *only* in the workplace. In this sensitivity analysis risks were calculated for exposure either only at home or only at work. This example illustrates the impact of altering exposure time on the risk estimates and the methodology which could be used to consider other alternative exposure times.

If exposure does not occur at work, and the time spent at work is 2000 hours per year, the time spent in a radon-bearing environment would be approximately equal to:

$$(8760 \text{ hours/year} - 2000 \text{ hours/year}) \cdot 0.9 \text{ indoor occupancy}$$
$$= 6084 \text{ hours/year}$$

This represents a 30% decrease [(8760–6084)/8760] in potential exposure time. Consequently, the WLMs for the general population shown in Table 8.5 were reduced by 30%, and are listed in Table 8.7 in column 2. (The original exposure values from Table 8.5 are listed in column 1.) The exposure values which result from this reduction in exposure time may also be appropriate to schoolchildren exposed at home but not in school.

A similar calculation for individuals exposed only at work (2000 hours/year) results in a 77% decrease [(8760–2000)/8760] in exposure. The values obtained by this modification are shown in column 3 of Table 8.7. The original probabilities from Table 8.6 and the probabilities calculated for adjusted exposures are shown in columns 4, 5, and 6 of Table 8.7.

In the exposure range governed by the linear probability equation, 0 to 26.8 WLM, changes in exposure result in a proportional change (30% or 77%) in the lifetime probabilities of lung cancer (P). At higher exposures, exposure time reductions result in nonproportional smaller decreases in risk. For example, at 2110 WLMs, a 30% decrease in exposure produces a 13% decrease in lung cancer risk and a 77% decrease in exposure results in a 34% decrease in risk. Varying exposure assumptions yield risks which are significantly lower than the original estimates. However, they continue to be relatively high.

Using this example as an illustration of how exposure time can be modified and used in equations to derive alternate risk estimates, various other exposure time assumptions could be considered, such as lifespan and the proportion of life spent in a building with a high or low radon level. This sensitivity analysis has dealt with one of the potential sources of variation in the risk estimate. Unfortunately, most sources of variation or error cannot be quantified, e.g., the effect of age at first exposure, smoking, dose rate, and latent period. Although one cannot assign a numerical value to the potential variation they may introduce, these factors may have a more significant effect on actual risk levels than those which can be quantitatively evaluated.

Table 8.7. Probability of Lung Cancer Due to Modified Daily Radon and Radon Daughter Exposure

Original Exposure Levels (WLMs)[a]	Home Exposure Only (30% decrease in exposure)	Work Exposure Only (77% decrease in exposure)	Original Probability[b]	Lifetime Probability: Home Exposure Only[c]	Lifetime Probability: Work Exposure Only[d]
7	4.9	1.6	$6.2 \cdot 10^{-3}$ (I)	$4.3 \cdot 10^{-3}$ (I)	$1.4 \cdot 10^{-3}$ (I)
70	49	16.1	$5.2 \cdot 10^{-2}$ (II)	$3.9 \cdot 10^{-2}$ (II)	$1.4 \cdot 10^{-2}$ (I)
870	609	200.1	$1.2 \cdot 10^{-1}$ (III)	$1.1 \cdot 10^{-1}$ (III)	$9.4 \cdot 10^{-2}$ (III)
1507	1054.9	346.6	$1.4 \cdot 10^{-1}$ (III)	$1.2 \cdot 10^{-1}$ (III)	$9.9 \cdot 10^{-2}$ (III)

[a] Values taken from Table 8.5.
[b] Original probabilities shown in Table 8.6. Equation numbers shown in parentheses.
[c] Values in column 2 used in equations in Table 8.4. Equation numbers shown in parentheses.
[d] Values in column 3 used in equations in Table 8.4. Equation numbers shown in parentheses.

8.4   ACCEPTABLE EXPOSURES

Using the method discussed in Chapter 6, the acceptable exposure based upon acceptable individual risk was determined. Let the level of exposure needed to produce a lung cancer risk of one lung cancer case per 100,000 exposed individuals (10^{-5}) be defined as acceptable. The probability equation relevant to a calculation of risk of $P = 10^{-5}$ is $P = 8.84 \cdot 10^{-4}$ (E) (see Equation I, Table 8.4). When 10^{-5} is substituted for P in the equation and solved for E, the resulting lifetime exposure is 0.0113 WLM ($1 \cdot 10^{-5} = 8.84 \cdot 10^{-4}$ E). The yearly exposure limit is 0.0113/75 years or 0.00015 WLM. Due to the large extrapolation necessary to calculate $P = 10^{-5}$, the estimate of acceptable exposure contains much greater uncertainty than the risk estimates in Table 8.6, which are based on very small or no extrapolations.

The acceptable level of risk can also be evaluated in terms of general radiation exposure limits, which are listed in Table 8.8. The conversion from WLM to rems is in the range of 8 to 20 rems/WLM.* Consequently, a radiation exposure limit for the general population of 0.5 rem/year results in a maximum exposure limit of 0.063 to 0.025 WLM/year (0.5/8 and 0.5/20). These levels are substantially *higher* than 0.00015 WLM/year, calculated above. However, since they are *lower* than the average yearly exposure of 0.116 WLM (see Table 8.1), they may not be practically attainable.

Table 8.8.   Radiation Exposure Limits

Type of Exposure	Federal Radiation Council[a]	National Council on Radiation Protection[b]
General population		
a. Individual	0.5 rem/year (whole body)	0.5 rem/year (whole body)
b. Average	5 rems/30 year (gonads)	0.17 rem/year (genetic) 0.17 rem/year (somatic)

[a]FRC, 1960
[b]NCRP, 1971

*The relationship between the exposure limits and radon and radon daughter exposure is not clear because of different conversion factors proposed for converting WLMs to rems. The differences are due to widely varying opinions on radon and radon daughter dosimetry. The following values have been suggested for rems per WLM: 8 (Jacobi and Eisfeld, 1981); 8–16 (BEIR, 1980); and 20 (UNSCEAR, 1977).

8.5   COMPARISON OF RESULTS TO OTHER ESTIMATES OF RISK

Epidemiologists and health physicists who have estimated lung cancer risks due to radon and radon daughter exposure share a common assumption: that the effectiveness of exposure in inducing lung cancer is constant over a broad range of exposures. Reliance on this assumption has led to underestimates of the lung cancer risks. A summary of several risk factors (in units of risk per WLM) is shown in Table 8.9. The use of a single risk factor for all exposure levels can be erroneous when the risk factor is a function of exposure. The risk attributable to a WLM of exposure is considered by some researchers to be the same, regardless of the cumulative exposure, e.g., 10 or 1000 WLMs. This reflects the underlying assumption that one unit of exposure has the same effectiveness in inducing lung cancer at all cumulative exposure levels. The risk factor analysis using RRC, which was presented in Section 8.2.4, indicates that this is probably not the case (see Figure 8.1).

The values in Table 8.9 were based upon data from relatively high-exposure epidemiological studies, where radiation effectiveness is lowest with respect to lung cancer induction. Consequently, risk factors were low. Although some moderate exposure level data were available, such as the Czechoslovakian study data, the lowest available data points were not preferentially used to estimate risks. The exposure levels of subjects in the Colorado epidemiological study used for extrapolation had cumulative exposure levels as high as 3720 WLMs (BEIR, 1980). By inspection of Figure 8.1b it is clear that linear extrapolation from Colorado data points through the origin results in a lower risk estimate at 25 WLMs than that obtained by an extrapolation through the origin from the Swedish data. This would be expected, based on decreased effectiveness of the radiation at higher exposures.

The risk factors shown in Table 8.9 should *only* have been used to estimate risks for exposures at comparably high levels, unless safety factors were used to account for potential risk underestimates. The hazards of high to low dose extrapolation are illustrated by comparing previous risk estimates with the results of this risk assessment. Extrapolations based on high-exposure epidemiological data have been shown to underestimate risks in those regions for which we now have data. The risk factors in Table 8.9 yield risks of 5.6×10^{-5} to 1.7×10^{-2} for 26.8 WLM cumulative exposure. This is based on the risk factors of 2.1×10^{-6} from Myers and Stewart (1979) and 6.5×10^{-4} from Thomas and McNeill (1982). The observed epidemiological data in Table 8.3 indicate an *actual* risk of 2.4×10^{-2} for 26.8 WLM cumulative exposure. Based on the

Table 8.9. Alternative Risk Factors for Lung Cancer Due to Radon and Radon Daughter Exposure

Lung Cancer Risk Factor[a]	Reference	Epidemiological Basis for Calculation
$2.1 \cdot 10^{-6} - 5.4 \cdot 10^{-5}$	Myers and Stewart, 1979	Colorado miners
$6.3 \cdot 10^{-6} - 1.6 \cdot 10^{-4}$	Myers and Stewart, 1979	Czechoslovakian miners
$1.0 \cdot 10^{-5} - 5.0 \cdot 10^{-4}$	Jacobi and Eisfeld, 1980	All available studies
$1.0 \cdot 10^{-5} - 4.0 \cdot 10^{-4}$	Cross et al., 1984	All available studies
$1.0 \cdot 10^{-4}$	Evans et al., 1981	All available studies
$3.8 \cdot 10^{-5}$	UNSCEAR, 1977	Colorado miners
$1.7 \cdot 10^{-4}$	UNSCEAR, 1977	Czechoslovakian miners (preventilation, hence higher exposure levels)
$2.3 \cdot 10^{-4}$	UNSCEAR, 1977	Czechoslovakian miners (postventilation)
$4.5 \cdot 10^{-4}$	UNSCEAR, 1977	Czechoslovakian miners (adjusted for latency)
$2.0 - 4.5 \cdot 10^{-4}$	UNSCEAR, 1977	All available studies
$1.0 - 2.0 \cdot 10^{-4}$	NCRP, 1984	All available studies
$6.5 \cdot 10^{-4}$ (upper estimate)	Thomas and McNeill, 1982	All available studies
$1.7 \cdot 10^{-4}$	ICRP, 1981	All available studies
$1.0 - 6.0 \cdot 10^{-4}$	Atomic Energy Control Board, 1982	All available studies

[a]Probability of lung cancer per WLM.

actual risk, the risk factors in Table 8.9 underestimated the risk at 26.8 WLM by as much as a factor of 429.

This risk assessment demonstrated that varying risk factors were appropriate at different cumulative exposures (see Figure 8.1a). In the experimental range (greater than 26.8 WLM) the exposure-risk relationship is best expressed in a more complex manner (see equations in Table 8.4) than the use of a single risk factor permits. The risk per WLM is dependent on the cumulative exposure. Table 8.10 shows risk factors (risk per WLM) at various exposures estimated by this risk assessment.

The comparison of this risk assessment's results to previous estimates provides an argument for using the most conservative risk extrapolation model in order that risks are not underestimated. This approach provides the greatest protection of the public's health. The comparison also indicates that the lowest available data point may yield the most appropriate risk estimate.

8.6 SOURCES OF UNCERTAINTY

As discussed in Chapter 1, there are numerous sources of uncertainty in a risk assessment. Most sources listed in Chapter 1 are applicable to this example. Those of particular concern are as follows:

- characterization of the general population and mining environments regarding radon daughter levels (most measurements made have been of radon only)
- characterization of the general population and mining environments with respect to environmental factors which may affect dosimetry (e.g., particle size and concentration, fraction of radon daughters attached to particles)
- lack of epidemiological exposure response data on subjects with the same age, sex, and proportion employed as the general population

Table 8.10. Lung Cancer Risks per Working Level Month

Working Level Months per Person	Lung Cancer Risk Factor	Equation Used[a]
1	$8.8 \cdot 10^{-4}$	I
10	$8.8 \cdot 10^{-4}$	I
100	$7 \cdot 10^{-4}$	II
1000	$1.2 \cdot 10^{-4}$	III
2500	$7 \cdot 10^{-5}$	III

[a]Equations from Table 8.4 were used to calculate the lung cancer risk.

- followup period and latency adjustment of Czechoslovakian and Colorado epidemiological study subjects
- antagonism or synergism of smoking or other environmental contaminants with radon and radon daughters

In addition, this risk assessment is limited because it focused on lung cancer as the only health effect of concern. Preliminary evidence exists that exposure to radon and radon daughters may increase the risk of stomach, bladder, and breast cancer (Fox et al., 1981; Radford and St. Clair Renard, 1984a; Bean, 1982). There may be increased risk associated with exposure to radon daughters, which are bone-seeking elements, among persons exposed during the early, bone-forming stages of growth. In addition, there are genetic risks associated with exposure to ionizing radiation which are difficult to detect and which may not be clearly manifest for many generations (BEIR, 1980).

As a result of the uncertainty inherent in this risk assessment, it is advisable to regard the calculated risks as minimum estimates. Consequently, the application of a safety factor would be justified to protect the public's health.

8.7 PUBLIC HEALTH AND REGULATORY IMPLICATIONS

The risks associated with radon and radon daughter exposure are relatively high for an environmental toxicant. At the exposure level considered to be a nationwide average — 9 WLM — the individual lifetime risk is estimated to be 6.2×10^{-3} (Tables 8.5 and 8.6). Based on this risk level, the portion of total lifetime lung cancer risk attributable to radon and its daughters is 8% for men and 18% for women. A lifetime lung cancer risk from all causes of 7.8×10^{-2} for men and 3.4×10^{-2} for women is assumed (see Table 4.5). Thus, exposure to radon and its daughters may contribute significantly to the overall lung cancer risks occurring in the United States.

The recommended maximum radon and radon daughter cumulative exposure given in Section 8.4 of 0.0113 WLM is considerably lower than the estimated average exposure of 9 WLM [based upon UNSCEAR data (UNSCEAR, 1982)]. Consequently, it is probably not practical to suggest that this level, which could be defined as acceptable or safe from the public health standard of one fatality per 100,000, is an appropriate cumulative exposure standard.

While elevated radon levels in indoor commercial and residential environments have only recently been identified on a large scale (UNSCEAR, 1977), there have already been some government actions taken to limit the exposure of the general population. In Sweden, where the radon levels are especially high (Alter, 1984), standards have been set for indoor levels of radon in homes for three categories of residences: new homes, homes undergoing renovation, and existing buildings. Sweden is the only country to date which has implemented a large-scale testing and regulatory program for control of radon levels. Recommendations, proposals, and standards put forth recently by other agencies and organizations, including the Atomic Energy Control Board of Canada, the National Institute of Radiological Protection (Sweden), the National Commission on Radiological Protection, the Union of Concerned Scientists, the Bonneville Power Administration, and the American Society of Heating, Refrigeration and Air Conditioning Engineers all yield a higher cumulative lifetime exposure than the acceptable exposure determined by this risk assessment of 0.0113 WLM (BPA, 1984; NIRP, 1984; Maine Department of Public Health, 1982).

To determine the practicality of reducing radon exposure levels significantly below those which now exist, a review of many factors would be required. These include: methods of reducing levels, their efficiency and cost, how such reductions would be financed and regulated, public information programs, and the relative effectiveness of the measures in reducing lung cancer risks. These considerations are beyond the scope of this example. While information is available on simple methods to reduce slightly elevated radon levels to an average level, this risk assessment suggests a more drastic reduction is needed. Information is not readily available on methods of reducing cumulative exposure to a level approaching 0.0113 WLM.

Methods for moderate reductions in radon and radon daughter levels include: increasing ventilation by opening windows and doors frequently or limiting weatherization, the use of air-to-air heat exchanges, and caulking and sealing holes and cracks in foundations. These are simple and relatively inexpensive (UNSCEAR, 1977; BPA, 1984).

It may be both practical and inexpensive to educate the public regarding this and other indoor air hazards. This type of approach has been used in the Pacific Northwest by the Bonneville Power Administration which initiated a program to provide information on health risks and methods of improving the indoor air quality to their residential customers (BPA, 1984). In Washington State legislation is being considered which requires public information and financial assistance programs to reduce exposure to radon and other indoor air pollutants through alterations in residential structures (House Bill 894, 1985).

Another approach which has been suggested is to conduct a large-scale survey of indoor environments to determine the extent of the radon problem. A survey could determine the scope of the problem by better defining average indoor levels. Unfortunately, other important questions could not be answered. Due to differences which occur on a building-by-building basis, in the soil and other materials near the foundation, very large differences can occur in the radon levels of adjacent structures. Architectural features, energy saving measures, and such insignificant housing characteristics as gaps in cement flooring of a basement also affect levels. Consequently, while a survey would provide a better general overview of the radon levels which exist, it would not have much predictive value for homes whose levels had not been measured. Building occupants would need measurement data on their structures to assess the need for remedial action. In many parts of the United States adequate information is available on radon levels to determine that risks *may* exist. These areas now need information on specific homes which have elevated radon levels. This can only be accomplished through measurements in each home. The cost to state or federal governments to undertake this type of survey would be high. An alternative would be to suggest, through the public education option discussed earlier, how inexpensive measurements can be obtained by individuals.

The public health and regulatory implications of the radon problem are complex due to the widespread occurrence of radon, and the relatively high risk levels associated with it. Current federal recommendations and standards for radon exposure do not reduce the lung cancer risks to levels traditionally defined as acceptable (less than 10^{-5}). The feasibility of reducing existing levels should be explored. Concurrently, programs to educate the public regarding simple, inexpensive measures they can take to reduce risks are advisable.

8.8 SUMMARY

This risk assessment determined that significant risks are associated with exposure to radon and its daughters at average and above average indoor exposure levels. Three epidemiological studies were used which provided exposure and response data in three different sections of the general population's exposure range. The studies varied in quality; however, the lowest exposure range, which is relevant to the majority of the population, was covered by a reliable experimental study of Swedish iron miners. Consequently, the risk estimates obtained in the low-exposure range are expected to be good predictors of risk.

Due to characteristics of the risk group, especially age at first exposure, which were not similar to the epidemiological group, the risk estimates may underestimate the levels of risk. In addition, this risk assessment dealt only with lung cancer risks; other types of risks may exist, including genetic risks and other cancers. Finally, the risk factor analysis, which employed the relative risk coefficient, indicated an increasing risk factor as the cumulative exposure decreased. Consequently, the risks at exposures in the subexperimental range may be greater than those predicted by the linear extrapolation method used. Based upon all of the above factors, the use of a safety factor in setting exposure limits may be appropriate.

8.9 CONCLUSIONS

This risk assessment example demonstrated methods which can be used when a relatively complicated risk scenario is being evaluated. The large exposure range of the risk group necessitated the use of three experimental studies. Risk estimates were made in both the experimental and subexperimental exposure ranges. It was necessary to make various types of adjustments for latency to compensate for the lack of adequate latency adjustments in two of the epidemiological studies. The calculation of exposure levels required the use of unusual radiological units unique to radon and radon daughter exposure.

The need to use more complex risk assessment methods will vary depending on the type of study which is undertaken and the experimental data base which is available. It is hoped that this example has given the risk assessor some insight into the methods presented in Chapters 2 through 6 and the modifications which can be made in those methods to accommodate the particular requirements of a risk assessment.

REFERENCES

ACGIH (American Conference of Governmental Industrial Hygienists), Documentation of Threshold Limit Values. Cincinnati, 1980.

ACGIH (American Conference of Governmental Industrial Hygienists), Threshold Limit Values for Chemical Substances and Physical Agents in the Work Environment and Biological Exposure Indices with Intended Changes for 1984–85. Cincinnati, OH.

Alter, W. Testimony at Hearings on Indoor Air Quality Research, Hearing before the Subcommittee on Energy Development and Application and the Subcommittee on Natural Resources and the Environment of the Committee on Science and Technology, United States House of Representatives, 98th Congress, August 2 and 3, 1983, #54. United States Government Printing Office, Washington, DC, 1984.

Altshuler, B. Modeling of dose-response relationships. *Environ. Health Pers.* 42:23–27, 1981.

Andrews, E. J., Ward, B. C., and Altman, N. H., Eds. *Spontaneous Animal Models of Human Disease.* Academic Press, New York, 1979.

Archer, V. E., and Lundin, F. E. Radiogenic lung cancer in man: Exposure-effect relationship. *Environ. Res.* 1:370–383, 1967.

Atomic Energy Control Board. Risk Estimate for Exposure to Alpha Emitters (ACRP-1) (INFO-0090), Advisory Committee on Radiological Protection. Ottawa, Canada, 1982.

Axelson, O., and Sundell, L. Mining, lung cancer and smoking. *Scand. J. Work Envir. Health.* 4:46–52, 1978.

Baetjer, A. M. Role of environmental temperature and humidity in susceptibility to disease. *Arch. Environ. Health.* 16:565–570, 1968.

Baum, J. W. Multiple simultaneous event model for radiation carcinogenesis. *Health Physics.* 25:97, 1973.

Bean, J. Drinking water and cancer incidence in Iowa II, radiation in drinking water. *J. Epidemiol.* 16:924–932, 1982.

BEIR Report. *The Effects on Populations of Exposures to Low Levels of Ionizing Radiation*: 1980. Committee on the Biological Effects of Ionizing Radiation, Division of Medical Sciences (BEIR III), National Academy Press, Washington, DC, 1980.

Bertig, L., and Stranden, E. Radon and radon daughters in mine atmospheres and influencing factors. In *Radiation Hazards in Mining Control, Measurement, and Medical Aspects*, M. Gomez, Ed., pp. 31–35. Society of Mining Engineers, New York, 1981.

BPA (Bonneville Power Administration), *Home Weatherization and Indoor Air Pollutants*. United States Department of Energy, Washington, DC, 1984.

Brown, L., Cliff, K. D., and Wrixon, A. D. *Natural Radiation Exposure Indoors*, Radiological Protection Bulletin No. 41. National Radiological Protection Board, Chilton, England, 1981.

Brown, L., Driscoll, A., Green, B. M., and Miles, J. C. *Pilot Study for Natural Radiation Survey*, Radiological Protection Bulletin No. 52. National Radiological Protection Board, Chilton, England, 1983.

Brown, N. A., and Fabro, S. The value of animal teratogenicity testing for predicting human risk. *Clin. Obstet. Gynecol.* 26:467–477, 1983.

Carlborg, F. W. Dose-response functions in carcinogenesis and the Weibull model. *Food. Cosmet. Toxicol.* 19:255–263, 1981a.

Carlborg, F. W. Multi-stage dose-response models in carcinogenesis. *Food. Cosmet. Toxicol.* 19:361–365, 1981b.

CFR (Code of Federal Regulations). Title 9 Subchapter A, Animal Welfare, Office of the Federal Register, Washington, DC, 1984.

Chameaud, J. R., Perraud, R., Masse, J., Nenot, J. C., and Lafuma, J. Cancers du poumon provoques chez le rat par le radon et ses descendents a diverses concentrations. *Proc. IAEA*, Chicago, 1977.

Chen, E. Tables of the cumulative binomial probability distribution, University of Illinois at Chicago, School of Public Health, personal communication, 1981.

Colton, T. *Statistics in Medicine*, Little, Brown, Boston, 1974.

Computation Laboratory, *Tables of the Cumulative Binomial Probability Distribution*. Harvard University Press, Cambridge, MA, 1955.

Cross, F. T., Harley, N. H., and Hofmann, W. Health effects and risks from radon-222 in drinking water. In *National Workshop on Radioactivity in Drinking Water, Committee Issue Papers*. U.S. Environmental Protection Agency, Washington, DC, 1984.

Crouch, E., and Wilson, R. Interspecies comparison of carcinogenic potency. *J. Toxicol. Environ. Health.* 5:1095–1118, 1979.

Crouch, E. A. C., and Wilson, R. Inter-Risk Comparisons. In *Assessment and Management of Chemical Risks*, ACS Symposium Series 239, J. V. Rodricks and R. G. Tardiff, Eds., pp. 97–112. American Chemical Society, Washington, DC, 1984.

Cunliffe-Beamer, T. L., Freeman, L. C., and Meyers, D. D. Barbiturate sleeptime in mice exposed to autoclaved or unautoclaved wood beddings. *Lab. Animal Sci.* 31(6):672–675, 1981.

DeCoufle, P., Thomas, T. L., and Pickle, L. W. Comparison of the proportionate mortality ratio and standardized mortality ratio risk measures. *Am. J. Epidemiol.* 111:263–269, 1980.

Dourson, M. L., and Stara, J. F. Regulatory history and experimental support of uncertainty (safety) factors. *Regulatory Toxicol. Pharmacol.* 3:224–238, 1983.

Edling, C., and Axelson, O. Quantitative aspects of radon daughter exposure and lung cancer in underground miners. *Brit. J. Ind. Med.* 40:182–187, 1983.

Evans, R. D., Harley, J. H., Jacobi, W., McLean, A. A., Mills, W. A., and Stewart, C. G. Estimates of risk from environmental exposure to radon-222 and its decay products. *Nature.* 290:98–100, 1981.

FDA (Food and Drug Administration). Chemical Compounds in Food-Producing Animals; Criteria and Procedures for Evaluating Assays for Carcinogenic Residues. *Federal Register.* 44:17070–17114, 1979.

FDA (Food and Drug Administration). Cosmetics; Proposed Ban on the Use of Methylene Chloride as an Ingredient of Aerosol Cosmetic Products. *Federal Register.* 50:51551–51559, 1985a.

FDA (Food and Drug Administration). Sponsored Chemicals in Food-Producing Animals; Criteria and Procedures for Evaluating the Safety of Carcinogenic Residues. *Federal Register.* 50:45530–45553, 1985b.

Fleischer, R. L., Mogro-Campero, A., and Turner, L. G. Indoor Radon Levels in the Northeastern United States: Effects of Energy Efficiency in Homes. Report No. 81 CRD 204, General Electric Technical Information Series. Technical Information Exchange, Schenectady, New York, 1981.

Fleiss, J. L. *Statistical Methods for Rates and Proportions*, Wiley, New York, 1973.

Fox, A. J., Goldblatt, P., and Kinlen, L. J. A study of the mortality of Cornish tin miners. *Brit. J. Ind. Med.* 38:378–380, 1981.

FRC (Federal Radiation Council). *Background Material for the Development of Radiation Protection Standards*, Staff Report #1. Washington, DC, 1960.

Freese, E. Thresholds in toxic, teratogenic, mutagenic, and carcinogenic effects. *Environ. Health Pers.* 6:171–178, 1973.

GAO (U.S. General Accounting Office) *Probabilistic Risk Assessment: An Emerging Aid to Nuclear Power Plant Safety Regulation*, GAO/RCED-85-11, June 19, 1985.

Gaylor, D. W., and Kodell, R. L. Linear interpolation algorithm for low dose risk assessment of toxic substances. *J. Environ. Pathol. Toxicol.* 4:305–312, 1980.

Gaylor, D. W., and Shapiro, R. E. Extrapolation and risk estimation for carcinogenesis. In *Advances in Modern Toxicology Volume 1, New Concepts in Safety Evaluation Part 2*, M. A. Mehlman, R. E. Shapiro, and H. Blumenthal, Eds., pp. 65–85. Hemisphere, New York, 1979.

Geber, W. F., Anderson T. A., and VanDyne, B. Physiological responses of the albino rat to chronic noise stress. *Arch. Environ. Health.* 12:751–754, 1966.

Geddes, D. M. The natural history of lung cancer: A review based on rates of tumor growth. *Brit. J. Dis. Chest.* 73:1–17, 1979.

George, A. C. Characterization of radon levels in indoor air. Report 82-48, presented at Air Pollution Control Association Meeting, New Orleans, 1982.

George, A. C., and Breslin, A. J. The distribution of ambient radon and radon daughters in residential buildings in the New Jersey-New York area. *Natural Radiation Environment III*, Vol. 2, T. F. Gesell and W. M. Lowder, Eds., pp. 1272–1307. U.S. Department of Energy, Washington, DC, 1980.

Gold, L. S., Sawyer, C. B., Magaw, R., Backman, G. M., deVeciana, M., Levinson, R., Hopper, N. K., Havender, W. R., Bernstein, L., Peto, R., Pike, M. C., and Ames, B. N. A carcinogenic potency database of the standardized results of animal bioassays. *Environ. Health Pers.* 58:9–319, 1984.

Gottlieb, L. S., and Husen, L. A. Lung cancer among Navajo uranium miners. *Chest.* 81:449–452, 1982.

Hallenbeck, W. H., and Cunningham-Burns, K. M. *Pesticides and Human Health*, Springer-Verlag, New York, 1985.

Hays, W. L. *Statistics*, 3rd edition, Holt, Reinhart, and Winston, New York, 1981.

Hegreberg G., and Leathers, C., Eds. *Bibliography of Induced Animal Models of Human Disease*. Washington State University, Pullman, WA, 1981.

Hegreberg, G., and Leathers, C., Eds. *Bibliography of Naturally Occur-*

ring Animal Models of Human Disease. Washington State University, Pullman, WA, 1981.

Hess, C. T., Weiffenback, C. V., and Norton, S. A. Variations of airborne and waterborne radon-222 in houses in Maine. *Environ. Int.* 8:59–66, 1982.

Hoel, D. G. Incorporation of background in dose-response models. *Fed. Proc.* 39:73–75, 1980.

Hoel, D. G., Gaylor, D. W., Kirschstein, R. L., Saffiotti, U., and Schneiderman, M. A. Estimation of risks of irreversible, delayed toxicity. *J. Toxicol. Environ. Health.* 1:133–151, 1975.

Hofmann, W. Steinhausler, F., and Pohl, E. Age, sex and weight-dependent dose patterns due to inhaled natural radionuclides. In *Natural Radiation Environment III*, Vol. 2, T. F. Gesell and W. M. Lowder, Eds., pp. 1116–1144. U.S. Department of Energy, Washington, DC, 1980.

Hogan, M. D. Extrapolation of animal carcinogenicity data: limitations and pitfalls. *Environ. Health Pers.* 47:333–337, 1983.

Hogan, M. D., and Hoel, D. G. Extrapolation to Man. In *Principles and Methods of Toxicology* A. W. Hayes, Ed., pp. 711–731. Raven Press, New York, 1982.

House Bill 894, State of Washington, 49th Legislature, 1985 Regular Session, Washington State House of Representatives. Olympia, Washington, 1985.

Hutt, P. B. Legal Considerations in Risk Assessment Under Federal Regulatory Statutes. In *Assessment and Management of Chemical Risks*, J. V. Rodricks and R. G. Tardiff, Eds., pp. 83–95. ACS Symposium Series 239, American Chemical Society, Washington, DC, 1984.

IARC (International Agency for Research on Cancer), *IARC Monographs on the Evaluation of the Carcinogenic Risk of Chemicals to Humans*, Vol. 33, World Health Organization, Lyon, France, 1984.

ICRP (International Commission on Radiological Protection), *Report of the Task Group on Reference Man*, No. 23, Pergamon Press, Elmsford, NY, 1975.

ICRP (International Commission on Radiological Protection), Limits for Inhalation of Radon Daughters by Workers, ICRP Publication 32, Annals of ICRP, 6. Pergamon Press, Elmsford, NY, 1981.

IRLG (Interagency Regulatory Liaison Group: EPA, CPSC, FDA, and OSHA), Scientific bases for identification of potential carcinogens and estimation of risks. *J. Nat. Cancer Inst.* 63:241–268, 1979.

Jacobi, W., and Eisfeld, K. *Dose to Tissues and Effective Dose Equivalent by Inhalation of Radon-222, Radon-220 and Their Short-lived*

Daughters, GSF Report S-626. National Technical Information Service, Springfield, VA, 1980.

Jacobi, W., and Eisfeld, K. Internal dosimetry of inhaled radon daughters. In *Radiation Hazards in Mining, Control Measurement, and Medical Aspects*, M. Gomez, Ed., pp. 31–35. Society of Mining Engineers, New York, 1981.

Jick, H., and Miettinen, O. S. Coffee and myocardial infarction, *New Eng. J. Med.* 289:63, 1973.

Johassen, N., and McLaughlin, J. P. Air filtration and radon daughter levels. *International Symposium on Indoor Air Pollution*, pp. 1–12. Amherst, MA, October, 1981.

Kasuda, T., Silberstein, S., and McNall, P. E. Modeling of radon and its daughter concentrations in ventilated spaces. *J. Air Poll. Control Assoc.* 30:1201–1207, 1980.

Krewski, D., and Van Ryzin, J. Dose Response Models for Quantal Response Toxicity Data. In *Statistics and Related Topics*, M. Csorgo, D. A. Dawson, J. N. K. Rao, A. K. Md. E. Saleh, Eds., pp. 201–231. North Holland, New York, 1981.

Kunz, E., Sevc, J., and Placek, V. L. Lung cancer mortality in uranium miners (methodological aspects). *Health Physics.* 35:579–580, 1978.

Kunz, E., Sevc, J., Placek, V., and Horacek, J. Lung cancer in man in relation to different time distributions of radiation exposure. *Health Physics.* 36:699–706, 1979.

Lundin, F. E., Wagoner, J. K., and Archer, V. E. *Radon Daughter Exposure and Respiratory Cancer, Quantitative and Temporal Effects.* Joint Monograph #1. U.S. Department of Health, Education and Welfare, Washington, DC, 1971.

Maine Department of Public Health. *Radon in Homes.* Augusta, ME, 1982.

Mantel, N., and Bryan, W. R. Safety testing of carcinogenic agents. *J. Nat. Cancer Inst.* 27:455–470, 1961.

Mattson, D. E. *Statistics Difficult Concepts, Understandable Explanations*, Mosby, St. Louis, 1981.

Mausner, J. S., and Bahn, A. K. *Epidemiology, An Introductory Text.* W. B. Saunders, Philadelphia, 1974.

Mays, C. W., Spiess, H., and Gerspach, A. Skeletal effects following radium-224 injections into humans. *Health Physics* 35:285–289, 1978.

Mitruka, B. M., Rawnsley, H. M., and Vadehra, D. V. *Animals for Medical Research: Models for the Study of Human Disease.* Wiley, New York, 1976.

Munro, I. C., and Krewski, D. R. Risk assessment and regulatory decision making. *Food. Cosmet. Toxicol.* 19:549–560, 1981.

Myers, D. K., and Stewart, C. G. *AECL-5970.* Chalk River Nuclear Laboratories, Chalk River, Canada, 1979.

Najarian, T. The controversy over the health effects of radiation. *Technol. Rev.*, pp. 74–82, November, 1978.

NAS (National Academy of Sciences), *Drinking Water and Health*, Safe Drinking Water Committee, Advisory Center on Toxicology, National Research Council, Washington, 1977.

Nayfield, K. C., and Besch, E. L. Comparative responses of rabbits and rats to elevated noise. *Lab. Animal Sci.* 31(4):386–390, 1981.

NCRP (National Council on Radiation Protection and Measurements). *Basic Radiation Protection Criteria.* Washington, DC, 1971.

NCRP (National Council on Radiation Protection and Measurements). *Evaluation of Occupational and Environmental Exposure to Radon and Radon Daughters in the United States*, NCRP Report 78. Bethesda, MD, 1984.

Newberne, P. M. Influence on pharmacological experiments of chemicals and other factors in diets of laboratory animals. *Fed. Proc.* 34(2):209–218, 1975.

NIH (National Institutes of Health), *Guide for the Care and Use of Laboratory Animals*, U.S. DHHS, Washington, DC, 1985.

NIRP (National Institute of Radiological Protection), *Radon in Housing* (84-10). Stockholm, Sweden, 1984.

NRC (National Research Council), *Risk Assessment in the Federal Government: Managing the Process*, National Academy Press, Washington, DC, 1983.

NRC (Nuclear Regulatory Commission). Proposed Standards for Protection Against Radiation. *Federal Register* 51:1092–1216, 1986.

OSHA (Occupational Safety and Health Administration), Identification, Classification, and Regulation of Potential Occupational Carcinogens. *Federal Register.* 45:5002–5296, 1980.

OSHA (Occupational Safety and Health Administration), Occupational Exposure to Ethylene Oxide. *Federal Register.* 48:17284–17319, 1983.

OSHA (Occupational Safety and Health Administration), Occupational Exposure to Benzene. *Federal Register.* 50:50512–50586, 1985.

OSTP (Office of Science and Technology Policy), Chemical Carcinogens; A Review of the Science and its Associated Principles. *Federal Register.* 50:10372–10442, 1985.

OTA (Office of Technology Assessment), *Cancer Testing Technology and Saccharin*, U.S. Government Printing Office, Washington, 1977.

Partridge, J. E., Horton, T. R., and Sensitaffar, E. L. *A Study of Radon-222 Released from Water during Typical Household Activi-*

ties, ORP/EERF-79-1. Office of Radiological Programs, USEPA, Washington, DC, 1979.

Pearson, E. S., and Hartley, H. O., editors, *Biometrika Tables for Statisticians*, vol. 1, Cambridge University Press, 1966.

Peterson, E. A., Augenstein, J. S., Tane's, D.C., and Augenstein, D. G. Noise raises blood pressure without impairing auditory sensitivity. *Science*. 211:1450–1452, 1981.

Pritchard, H. M., Gesell, T. F., Hess, C. T., and Weiffenbach, N. P. The Association between grab samples and integrated radon measurements in dwellings in Texas and Maine. *Environ. Int'l*. 8:83–87, 1982.

Radford, E. P., and St. Clair Renard, K. G. Lung cancer in Swedish iron miners exposed to low doses of radon daughters. *New England J. Med*. 310:1485–1494, 1984a.

Radford, E. P., and St. Clair Renard, K. G. Application of studies of miners to radon problem in homes. Presented at the Third International Conference on Indoor Air Quality and Control. Stockholm, Sweden, August, 1984b.

Rodricks, J., and Taylor, M. R. Application of risk assessment to food safety decision making. *Regulatory Toxicol. Pharmacol*. 3:275–307, 1983.

Rossi, H. H., and Kellerer, A. M. Radiation carcinogenesis at low doses. *Science* 175:200, 1972.

Rundo, J., and Toohey, R. E. Radon in houses — A review. In *Radiological and Environmental Research Division Annual Report, Center for Human Radiobiology, ANL-81-85, Part II*, p. 101. Argonne National Laboratory, Argonne, Illinois, 1981.

Rundo, J., and Toohey, R. E. Radon in homes and other technologically enhanced radioactivity. In *Environmental Research Division Annual Report, Center for Human Radiobiology, July 1982–June 1983, ANL 83-100, Part II*, pp. 35–337. National Technical Information Service, Springfield, VA, 1984.

Rundo, J., Markun, F., May, H. A., and Plondke, D. J. Some measurements of radon and its daughters in house. In *Radiological and Environmental Research Division Annual Report, Center for Human Radiobiology, ANL 79-65, Part II*, pp. 1–12. Argonne National Laboratory, Argonne, Illinois, 1979.

Samet, J. M., Dutvirt, D. M. Waxweiler, R. F., and Key, C. R. Uranium mining and lung cancer in Navajo men. *New England J. Med*. 310:1481–1484, 1984.

Sansone, E. B., and Losikoff, A. M. Potential contamination from feeding test chemicals in carcinogen bioassay research: evaluation of single and double corridor animal housing facilities. *Toxicol. Appl. Pharmacol.* 50:115-121, 1979.

SEER Program: Cancer Incidence and Mortality in the U.S. 1973-81, USDHHS, PHS, NIH, Biometry Branch, Division of Cancer Prevention and Control, NIH No. 85-1837, Bethesda, 1984.

Seidman, H., Mushivski, M. H., Gelb, S. K., and Silverberg, E. Probabilities of eventually developing or dying of cancer—U.S., 1985. *CA-A Cancer J. Clinicians.* 35:36-56, 1985.

Sevc, J. E., Kunz, E., and Placek, V. Lung cancer in uranium miners and long term exposure to radon daughter products. *Health Physics.* 30:433-437, 1976.

Snihs, J. O. Significance of radon and its progeny as natural radiation sources in Sweden. In *Noble Gases, Symposium Conference 730915*, R. E. Stanley and A. A. Moghissi, Eds., pp. 115-130. U.S. Environmental Protection Agency, Washington, DC, 1973.

Staffa, J. A., and Mehlman, M. A., editors, *Innovations in Cancer Risk Assessment* (ED$_{01}$ Study). Pathotox, Park Forest South, IL, 1979.

Steinhausler, F. Radon-222 and lead-214 build up over time indoors. *Health Physics* 29:705, 1975.

Theiss, J. C. The ranking of chemicals for carcinogenic potency. *Regulatory Toxicol. Pharmacol.* 3:320-328, 1983.

Thomas, D. C., and McNeill, K. G. *Risk Estimates for the Health Effects of Alpha Radiation*, INFO-0081. Atomic Energy Control Board of Canada, Ottawa, Ontario, 1982.

UNSCEAR (United Nations Scientific Committee on the Effects of Atomic Radiation), *Sources and Effects of Ionizing Radiation.* UNSCEAR 1977 Report. United Nations, New York, 1977.

UNSCEAR (United Nations Scientific Committee on the Effects of Atomic Radiation), *Ionizing Radiation; Sources and Biological Effects.* 1982 Report to the General Assembly, with Annexes. United Nations, New York, 1982.

Upton, A. C. Biological aspects of radiation carcinogenesis. In *Radiation Carcinogenesis: Epidemiology and Biological Significance*, J. D. Boice and J. F. Fraumeni, Eds., pp. 18-35. Raven Press, New York, 1984.

USDOC (U.S. Department of Commerce, Bureau of the Census), *Statistical Abstracts of the U.S. 1981*, 102d edition, U.S. Government Printing Office, Washington, DC, 1981.

USEPA (U.S. Environmental Protection Agency) Guidelines and Methodology Used in the Preparation of Health Effect Assessment Chapters of the Consent Decree Water Criteria Documents. *Federal Register* 45:79347-79357, 1980.

USEPA (U.S. Environmental Protection Agency) Proposed Guidelines for Carcinogen, Mutagenicity, and Developmental Toxicant Risk Assessment. *Federal Register* 49:46294–46331, 1984.

USEPA (U.S. Environmental Protection Agency) *Federal Register*, National Primary Drinking Water Regulations; Volatile Synthetic Organic Chemicals; Final Rule and Proposed Rule (50:46830–46901, 1985). National Primary Drinking Water Regulations, Synthetic Organic Chemicals, Inorganic Chemicals and Microorganisms; Proposed Rule. (50:46936–47025, 1985).

Van Ryzin, J. Quantitative risk assessment. *J. Occ. Med.* 22:321–326, 1980.

Vesell, E. S. Induction of drug-metabolizing enzymes in liver microsomes of mice and rats by softwood bedding. *Science.* 157:1057–1058, 1967.

Wagoner, J. K., Archer, V. E., Lundin, F. E., Holaday, D. A., and Lloyd, J. W. Radiation as a cause of lung cancer among uranium miners. *New England J. Med.* 273:181–187, 1965.

Wakabayashi, T., Kato, H., Ikeda, T., and Schull, W. J. Studies of the mortality of A-bomb survivors, Report 7. Part III. Incidence of cancer in 1959–1978 based on the tumor registry, Nagasaki. *Radiation Res.* 93:112–146, 1983.

Walrath, J., and Fraumeni, J. F. Proportionate Mortality Among New York Embalmers. In *Formaldehyde Toxicity*, J. E. Gibson, Ed., pp. 227–236. Hemisphere, New York, 1983.

Whittemore, A. S., and McMillan, A. Lung cancer mortality among U. S. uranium miners, a reappraisal. *J. Nat. Cancer Inst.* 71:489-499, 1983.

Wilson, B. J., Ed. *The Radiochemical Manual*, 2nd ed., Radiochemical Center, Amersham, England, 1966.

Wong, O. An epidemiologic mortality study of a cohort of chemical workers potentially exposed to formaldehyde, with a discussion on SMR and PMR. In *Formaldehyde Toxicity*, J. E. Gibson, Ed., pp. 256–272, Hemisphere, New York, 1983.

Zentner, R. D. Chemical Industry Perspectives on Regulatory Impact Analysis. In *Assessment and Management of Chemical Risks*, J. V. Rodricks and R. G. Tardiff, Eds., pp. 161–173. ACS Symposium Series 239, American Chemical Society, Washington, DC, 1984.

Zondek, B., and Tamari, I. Effect of audiogenic stimulation on genital function and reproduction III: Infertility induced by auditory stimuli prior to mating, *Acta Endocrinol.* 45 (Suppl. 90):227–234, 1964.

APPENDICES

APPENDIX 1

Lower 1% and Upper 99% Limits for a Binomial Variable

The lower 1% limits were calculated by the Harvard University Computation Laboratory (1955) from:

$$\sum_{i=X}^{N} {}_N C_i \, P^i \, (1-P)^{N-i} = 0.01$$

where $N = N_c$ = number of subjects in the control group
$X = X_c$ = number of cases observed in the control group
${}_N C_i = N!/[(N-i)!i!]$ = combination of N control subjects taken i at a time
$P = P'_c$ = lower 1% limit on control group response
$P_c = X_c/N_c$ = control group response

The upper 99% limits were calculated by Dr. Edwin Chen of the University of Illinois at Chicago (1981) from:

$$\sum_{i=o}^{X} {}_N C_i \, P^i \, (1-P)^{N-i} = 0.01$$

where $N = N_t$ = number of subjects in the test group
$X = X_t$ = number of cases observed in the test group
${}_N C_i = N!/[(N-i)!i!]$ = combination of N test subjects taken i at a time
$P = P'_t$ = upper 99% limit on test group response
$P_t = X_t/N_t$ = test group response

These limits are enumerated on the following pages.

APPENDIX 1 (cont.)

LOWER 1% LIMITS FOR A BINOMIAL VARIABLE

N_C	X_C	P_C'	N_C	X_C	P_C'	N_C	X_C	P_C'
10	2	.01	17	2	.01	22	3	.02
	3	.05		3	.03		4	.04
	4	.09		4	.05		5	.06
	5	.16		5	.08		6	.09
				6	.12		7	.12
11	2	.01		7	.15		8	.15
	3	.04		8	.20		9	.18
	4	.08					10	.21
	5	.13	18	2	.01		11	.25
				3	.02			
12	2	.01		4	.05	23	3	.02
	3	.04		5	.08		4	.04
	4	.08		6	.11		5	.06
	5	.12		7	.15		6	.08
	6	.17		8	.19		7	.11
				9	.23		8	.14
13	2	.01					9	.17
	3	.04	19	2	.01		10	.20
	4	.07		3	.02		11	.24
	5	.11		4	.05			
	6	.16		5	.07	24	3	.02
				6	.10		4	.04
14	2	.01		7	.14		5	.06
	3	.03		8	.17		6	.08
	4	.06		9	.21		7	.11
	5	.10					8	.13
	6	.16	20	3	.02		9	.16
	7	.19		4	.04		10	.19
				5	.07		11	.23
15	2	.01		6	.10		12	.26
	3	.03		7	.13			
	4	.06		8	.16	25	3	.02
	5	.09		9	.20		4	.03
	6	.13		10	.24		5	.05
	7	.18					6	.08
			21	3	.02		7	.10
16	2	.01		4	.04		8	.13
	3	.03		5	.06		9	.15
	4	.05		6	.09		10	.19
	5	.09		7	.12		11	.22
	6	.13		8	.15		12	.25
	7	.17		9	.19			
	8	.21		10	.23	26	3	.02
							4	.03

APPENDIX 1 (cont.)

LOWER 1% LIMITS FOR A BINOMIAL VARIABLE

N_c	X_c	P_c'	N_c	X_c	P_c'	N_c	X_c	P_c'
26	5	.05	29	12	.21	32	15	.26
	6	.07		13	.24		16	.29
	7	.10		14	.27			
	8	.12				33	3	.01
	9	.15	30	3	.01		4	.02
	10	.18		4	.03		5	.04
	11	.21		5	.04		6	.06
	12	.24		6	.06		7	.07
	13	.27		7	.08		8	.09
				8	.10		9	.11
27	3	.02		9	.13		10	.14
	4	.03		10	.15		11	.16
	5	.05		11	.18		12	.18
	6	.07		12	.20		13	.20
	7	.09		13	.23		14	.23
	8	.12		14	.26		15	.25
	9	.14		15	.28		16	.28
	10	.17						
	11	.20	31	3	.01	34	3	.01
	12	.23		4	.03		4	.02
	13	.26		5	.04		5	.04
				6	.06		6	.05
28	3	.01		7	.08		7	.07
	4	.03		8	.10		8	.09
	5	.05		9	.12		9	.11
	6	.07		10	.14		10	.13
	7	.09		11	.17		11	.15
	8	.11		12	.19		12	.17
	9	.14		13	.22		13	.20
	10	.16		14	.25		14	.22
	11	.19		15	.27		15	.25
	12	.22					16	.28
	13	.25	32	3	.01		17	.31
	14	.28		4	.03			
				5	.04	35	3	.01
29	3	.01		6	.06		4	.02
	4	.03		7	.08		5	.04
	5	.05		8	.10		6	.05
	6	.06		9	.12		7	.07
	7	.08		10	.14		8	.09
	8	.11		11	.16		9	.11
	9	.13		12	.19		10	.13
	10	.16		13	.21		11	.15
	11	.18		14	.24		12	.17

APPENDIX 1 (cont.)

LOWER 1% LIMITS FOR A BINOMIAL VARIABLE

N_c	X_c	P_c'	N_c	X_c	P_c'	N_c	X_c	P_c'
35	13	.19	38	7	.06	40	15	.21
	14	.21		8	.08		16	.23
	15	.24		9	.10		17	.25
	16	.26		10	.12		18	.27
	17	.29		11	.13		19	.29
				12	.15		20	.31
36	3	.01		13	.17			
	4	.02		14	.20	41	3	.01
	5	.04		15	.22		4	.02
	6	.05		16	.24		5	.03
	7	.07		17	.26		6	.04
	8	.08		18	.28		7	.06
	9	.10		19	.31		8	.07
	10	.13					9	.09
	11	.14	39	3	.01		10	.11
	12	.17		4	.02		11	.13
	13	.19		5	.03		12	.14
	14	.21		6	.05		13	.16
	15	.23		7	.06		14	.18
	16	.25		8	.08		15	.20
	17	.28		9	.10		16	.22
	18	.30		10	.11		17	.24
				11	.13		18	.26
37	3	.01		12	.15		19	.28
	4	.02		13	.17		20	.30
	5	.03		14	.19			
	6	.05		15	.21	42	3	.01
	7	.06		16	.23		4	.02
	8	.08		17	.25		5	.03
	9	.10		18	.28		6	.04
	10	.12		19	.30		7	.06
	11	.14					8	.07
	12	.16	40	3	.01		9	.09
	13	.18		4	.02		10	.10
	14	.20		5	.03		11	.12
	15	.22		6	.05		12	.14
	16	.25		7	.06		13	.16
	17	.27		8	.08		14	.17
	18	.29		9	.09		15	.19
				10	.11		16	.21
38	3	.01		11	.13		17	.23
	4	.02		12	.15		18	.25
	5	.03		13	.17		19	.27
	6	.05		14	.19		20	.29

APPENDIX 1 (cont.)

LOWER 1% LIMITS FOR A BINOMIAL VARIABLE

N_c	X_c	P_c'	N_c	X_c	P_c'	N_c	X_c	P_c'
42	21	.31	45	4	.02	47	5	.03
				5	.03		6	.04
43	3	.01		6	.04		7	.05
	4	.02		7	.05		8	.06
	5	.03		8	.07		9	.08
	6	.04		9	.08		10	.09
	7	.06		10	.10		11	.11
	8	.07		11	.11		12	.13
	9	.08		12	.13		13	.14
	10	.10		13	.14		14	.15
	11	.12		14	.16		15	.17
	12	.13		15	.18		16	.19
	13	.15		16	.20		17	.21
	14	.17		17	.22		18	.22
	15	.19		18	.23		19	.24
	16	.21		19	.25		20	.26
	17	.23		20	.27		21	.28
	18	.25		21	.29		22	.30
	19	.27		22	.31		23	.32
	20	.29						
	21	.31	46	3	.01	48	3	.01
				4	.02		4	.02
44	3	.01		5	.03		5	.03
	4	.02		6	.04		6	.04
	5	.03		7	.05		7	.05
	6	.04		8	.06		8	.06
	7	.05		9	.08		9	.08
	8	.07		10	.10		10	.09
	9	.08		11	.11		11	.10
	10	.10		12	.13		12	.12
	11	.12		13	.14		13	.13
	12	.13		14	.16		14	.15
	13	.15		15	.18		15	.17
	14	.17		16	.19		16	.19
	15	.19		17	.21		17	.20
	16	.20		18	.23		18	.22
	17	.22		19	.25		19	.24
	18	.24		20	.27		20	.25
	19	.26		21	.29		21	.27
	20	.28		22	.30		22	.29
	21	.30		23	.32		23	.31
	22	.32					24	.33
			47	3	.01			
45	3	.01		4	.02	49	3	.01

APPENDIX 1 (cont.)

LOWER 1% LIMITS FOR A BINOMIAL VARIABLE

N_c	X_c	P_c'	N_c	X_c	P_c'	N_c	X_c	P_c'
49	4	.02	50	25	.33	54	22	.25
	5	.03					23	.27
	6	.04	52	4	.01		24	.29
	7	.05		5	.02		25	.30
	8	.06		6	.03		26	.32
	9	.07		7	.05		27	.34
	10	.09		8	.06			
	11	.10		9	.07	56	4	.01
	12	.12		10	.08		5	.02
	13	.13		11	.10		6	.03
	14	.15		12	.11		7	.04
	15	.17		13	.13		8	.05
	16	.18		14	.14		9	.06
	17	.20		15	.15		10	.08
	18	.21		16	.17		11	.09
	19	.23		17	.19		12	.10
	20	.25		18	.20		13	.11
	21	.27		19	.22		14	.13
	22	.28		20	.23		15	.14
	23	.30		21	.25		16	.16
	24	.32		22	.27		17	.17
				23	.28		18	.19
50	3	.01		24	.30		19	.20
	4	.02		25	.32		20	.21
	5	.02		26	.33		21	.23
	6	.04					22	.24
	7	.05	54	4	.01		23	.26
	8	.06		5	.02		24	.28
	9	.07		6	.03		25	.29
	10	.09		7	.04		26	.31
	11	.10		8	.06		27	.32
	12	.12		9	.07		28	.34
	13	.13		10	.08			
	14	.14		11	.09	58	4	.01
	15	.16		12	.11		5	.02
	16	.18		13	.12		6	.03
	17	.19		14	.13		7	.04
	18	.21		15	.15		8	.05
	19	.23		16	.16		9	.06
	20	.24		17	.18		10	.07
	21	.26		18	.19		11	.08
	22	.28		19	.21		12	.10
	23	.29		20	.22		13	.11
	24	.31		21	.24		14	.13

APPENDIX 1 (cont.)

LOWER 1% LIMITS FOR A BINOMIAL VARIABLE

N_c	X_c	P_c'	N_c	X_c	P_c'	N_c	X_c	P_c'
58	15	.14	62	4	.01	64	19	.17
	16	.15		5	.02		20	.19
	17	.17		6	.03		21	.20
	18	.18		7	.04		22	.21
	19	.19		8	.05		23	.22
	20	.21		9	.06		24	.24
	21	.22		10	.07		25	.25
	22	.23		11	.08		26	.27
	23	.25		12	.09		27	.28
	24	.26		13	.10		28	.29
	25	.28		14	.11		29	.31
	26	.30		15	.13		30	.32
	27	.31		16	.14		31	.33
	28	.33		17	.15		32	.35
	29	.34		18	.17			
				19	.18	66	4	.01
60	4	.01		20	.19		5	.02
	5	.02		21	.20		6	.03
	6	.03		22	.22		7	.04
	7	.04		23	.23		8	.04
	8	.05		24	.25		9	.05
	9	.06		25	.26		10	.06
	10	.07		26	.27		11	.07
	11	.08		27	.29		12	.08
	12	.09		28	.30		13	.10
	13	.11		29	.32		14	.11
	14	.12		30	.33		15	.12
	15	.13		31	.34		16	.13
	16	.14					17	.14
	17	.16	64	4	.01		18	.15
	18	.17		5	.02		19	.17
	19	.19		6	.03		20	.18
	20	.20		7	.04		21	.19
	21	.21		8	.05		22	.20
	22	.23		9	.06		23	.22
	23	.24		10	.07		24	.23
	24	.26		11	.08		25	.24
	25	.27		12	.09		26	.26
	26	.28		13	.10		27	.27
	27	.30		14	.11		28	.28
	28	.31		15	.13		29	.30
	29	.33		16	.13		30	.31
	30	.35		17	.15		31	.32
				18	.16		32	.34

APPENDIX 1 (cont.)

LOWER 1% LIMITS FOR A BINOMIAL VARIABLE

N_c	X_c	P_c'	N_c	X_c	P_c'	N_c	X_c	P_c'
66	33	.35	70	14	.10	72	25	.22
				15	.11		26	.23
68	4	.01		16	.13		27	.25
	5	.02		17	.13		28	.26
	6	.03		18	.14		29	.27
	7	.03		19	.16		30	.28
	8	.04		20	.17		31	.29
	9	.05		21	.18		32	.31
	10	.06		22	.19		33	.32
	11	.07		23	.20		34	.33
	12	.08		24	.22		35	.35
	13	.09		25	.23		36	.36
	14	.10		26	.24			
	15	.12		27	.25	74	4	.01
	16	.13		28	.27		5	.02
	17	.14		29	.28		6	.02
	18	.15		30	.29		7	.03
	19	.16		31	.30		8	.04
	20	.17		32	.32		9	.05
	21	.19		33	.33		10	.06
	22	.20		34	.34		11	.07
	23	.21		35	.36		12	.08
	24	.22					13	.08
	25	.24	72	4	.01		14	.09
	26	.25		5	.02		15	.11
	27	.26		6	.02		16	.12
	28	.27		7	.03		17	.13
	29	.29		8	.04		18	.14
	30	.30		9	.05		19	.15
	31	.31		10	.06		20	.16
	32	.33		11	.07		21	.17
	33	.34		12	.08		22	.18
	34	.35		13	.09		23	.19
				14	.10		24	.20
70	4	.01		15	.11		25	.21
	5	.02		16	.12		26	.23
	6	.02		17	.13		27	.24
	7	.03		18	.14		28	.25
	8	.04		19	.15		29	.26
	9	.05		20	.16		30	.27
	10	.06		21	.17		31	.29
	11	.07		22	.19		32	.30
	12	.08		23	.20		33	.31
	13	.09		24	.21		34	.32

APPENDIX 1 (cont.)

LOWER 1% LIMITS FOR A BINOMIAL VARIABLE

N_c	X_c	P_c'	N_c	X_c	P_c'	N_c	X_c	P_c'
74	35	.33	78	8	.04	80	15	.10
	36	.35		9	.05		16	.11
	37	.36		10	.05		17	.12
				11	.06		18	.13
76	4	.01		12	.07		19	.14
	5	.02		13	.08		20	.15
	6	.02		14	.09		21	.16
	7	.03		15	.10		22	.17
	8	.04		16	.11		23	.18
	9	.05		17	.12		24	.19
	10	.06		18	.13		25	.20
	11	.06		19	.14		26	.21
	12	.07		20	.15		27	.22
	13	.08		21	.16		28	.23
	14	.09		22	.17		29	.24
	15	.10		23	.18		30	.25
	16	.11		24	.19		31	.26
	17	.13		25	.20		32	.27
	18	.13		26	.21		33	.28
	19	.14		27	.22		34	.30
	20	.15		28	.24		35	.31
	21	.17		29	.25		36	.32
	22	.18		30	.26		37	.33
	23	.19		31	.27		38	.34
	24	.20		32	.28		39	.35
	25	.21		33	.29		40	.37
	26	.22		34	.30			
	27	.23		35	.32	82	4	.01
	28	.24		36	.33		5	.01
	29	.25		37	.34		6	.02
	30	.27		38	.35		7	.03
	31	.28		39	.36		8	.03
	32	.29					9	.04
	33	.30	80	4	.01		10	.05
	34	.31		5	.01		11	.06
	35	.33		6	.02		12	.07
	36	.34		7	.03		13	.08
	37	.35		8	.04		14	.08
	38	.36		9	.04		15	.09
				10	.05		16	.10
78	4	.01		11	.06		17	.11
	5	.01		12	.07		18	.13
	6	.02		13	.08		19	.13
	7	.03		14	.09		20	.14

APPENDIX 1 (cont.)

LOWER 1% LIMITS FOR A BINOMIAL VARIABLE

N_c	X_c	P'_c	N_c	X_c	P'_c	N_c	X_c	P'_c
82	21	.15	84	26	.20	86	30	.23
	22	.16		27	.21		31	.24
	23	.17		28	.22		32	.25
	24	.18		29	.23		33	.26
	25	.19		30	.24		34	.27
	26	.20		31	.25		35	.28
	27	.21		32	.26		36	.29
	28	.22		33	.27		37	.31
	29	.23		34	.28		38	.32
	30	.24		35	.29		39	.33
	31	.26		36	.30		40	.34
	32	.27		37	.31		41	.35
	33	.28		38	.32		42	.36
	34	.29		39	.33		43	.37
	35	.30		40	.35			
	36	.31		41	.36	88	4	.01
	37	.32		42	.37		5	.01
	38	.33					6	.02
	39	.34	86	4	.01		7	.03
	40	.36		5	.01		8	.03
	41	.37		6	.02		9	.04
				7	.03		10	.05
84	4	.01		8	.03		11	.05
	5	.01		9	.04		12	.06
	6	.02		10	.05		13	.07
	7	.03		11	.06		14	.08
	8	.03		12	.06		15	.09
	9	.04		13	.07		16	.10
	10	.05		14	.08		17	.10
	11	.06		15	.09		18	.11
	12	.07		16	.10		19	.13
	13	.07		17	.11		20	.13
	14	.08		18	.12		21	.14
	15	.09		19	.13		22	.15
	16	.10		20	.13		23	.16
	17	.11		21	.14		24	.17
	18	.12		22	.15		25	.18
	19	.13		23	.17		26	.19
	20	.14		24	.17		27	.20
	21	.15		25	.18		28	.21
	22	.16		26	.19		29	.22
	23	.17		27	.20		30	.23
	24	.18		28	.21		31	.24
	25	.19		29	.22		32	.25

APPENDIX 1 (cont.)

LOWER 1% LIMITS FOR A BINOMIAL VARIABLE

N_C	X_C	P_C'	N_C	X_C	P_C'	N_C	X_C	P_C'
88	33	.26	90	35	.27	92	36	.27
	34	.27		36	.28		37	.28
	35	.28		37	.29		38	.29
	36	.29		38	.30		39	.30
	37	.30		39	.31		40	.31
	38	.31		40	.32		41	.32
	39	.32		41	.33		42	.33
	40	.33		42	.34		43	.34
	41	.34		43	.35		44	.35
	42	.35		44	.36		45	.36
	43	.36		45	.38		46	.38
	44	.37						
			92	4	.01	94	4	.01
90	4	.01		5	.01		5	.01
	5	.01		6	.02		6	.02
	6	.02		7	.02		7	.02
	7	.02		8	.03		8	.03
	8	.03		9	.04		9	.04
	9	.04		10	.04		10	.04
	10	.05		11	.05		11	.05
	11	.05		12	.06		12	.06
	12	.06		13	.07		13	.07
	13	.07		14	.08		14	.07
	14	.08		15	.08		15	.08
	15	.08		16	.09		16	.09
	16	.09		17	.10		17	.10
	17	.10		18	.11		18	.11
	18	.11		19	.12		19	.11
	19	.12		20	.13		20	.13
	20	.13		21	.13		21	.13
	21	.14		22	.14		22	.14
	22	.15		23	.15		23	.15
	23	.16		24	.16		24	.16
	24	.17		25	.17		25	.17
	25	.17		26	.18		26	.17
	26	.18		27	.19		27	.19
	27	.19		28	.20		28	.19
	28	.20		29	.21		29	.20
	29	.21		30	.22		30	.21
	30	.22		31	.23		31	.22
	31	.23		32	.24		32	.23
	32	.24		33	.24		33	.24
	33	.25		34	.25		34	.25
	34	.26		35	.26		35	.26

APPENDIX 1 (cont.)

LOWER 1% LIMITS FOR A BINOMIAL VARIABLE

N_c	X_c	P_c'	N_c	X_c	P_c'	N_c	X_c	P_c'
94	36	.27	96	36	.26	98	35	.25
	37	.28		37	.27		36	.26
	38	.29		38	.28		37	.27
	39	.30		39	.29		38	.27
	40	.31		40	.30		39	.28
	41	.32		41	.31		40	.29
	42	.33		42	.32		41	.30
	43	.33		43	.33		42	.31
	44	.35		44	.34		43	.32
	45	.36		45	.35		44	.33
	46	.37		46	.36		45	.34
	47	.38		47	.37		46	.35
				48	.38		47	.36
96	5	.01					48	.37
	6	.02	98	5	.01		49	.38
	7	.02		6	.02			
	8	.03		7	.02	100	5	.01
	9	.04		8	.03		6	.02
	10	.04		9	.04		7	.02
	11	.05		10	.04		8	.03
	12	.06		11	.05		9	.03
	13	.06		12	.06		10	.04
	14	.07		13	.06		11	.05
	15	.08		14	.07		12	.05
	16	.09		15	.08		13	.06
	17	.10		16	.08		14	.07
	18	.10		17	.09		15	.08
	19	.11		18	.10		16	.08
	20	.12		19	.11		17	.09
	21	.13		20	.12		18	.10
	22	.14		21	.13		19	.11
	23	.14		22	.13		20	.11
	24	.15		23	.14		21	.13
	25	.16		24	.15		22	.13
	26	.17		25	.16		23	.14
	27	.18		26	.17		24	.15
	28	.19		27	.18		25	.16
	29	.20		28	.19		26	.17
	30	.21		29	.19		27	.17
	31	.22		30	.20		28	.18
	32	.22		31	.21		29	.19
	33	.23		32	.22		30	.20
	34	.24		33	.23		31	.21
	35	.25		34	.24		32	.21

APPENDIX 1 (cont.)

LOWER 1% LIMITS FOR A BINOMIAL VARIABLE

N_c	X_c	P_c'	N_c	X_c	P_c'	N_c	X_c	P_c'
100	33	.22	110	30	.18	120	22	.11
	34	.23		31	.19		23	.11
	35	.24		32	.19		24	.12
	36	.25		33	.20		25	.13
	37	.26		34	.21		26	.13
	38	.27		35	.22		27	.14
	39	.28		36	.23		28	.15
	40	.29		37	.23		29	.16
	41	.30		38	.24		30	.17
	42	.30		39	.25		31	.17
	43	.31		40	.26		32	.18
	44	.32		41	.27		33	.19
	45	.33		42	.27		34	.19
	46	.34		43	.28		35	.20
	47	.35		44	.29		36	.21
	48	.36		45	.30		37	.21
	49	.37		46	.31		38	.22
	50	.38		47	.32		39	.23
				48	.33		40	.24
110	5	.01		49	.33		41	.24
	6	.01		50	.34		42	.25
	7	.02		51	.35		43	.26
	8	.03		52	.36		44	.27
	9	.03		53	.37		45	.27
	10	.04		54	.38		46	.28
	11	.04		55	.39		47	.29
	12	.05					48	.30
	13	.06	120	5	.01		49	.30
	14	.06		6	.01		50	.31
	15	.07		7	.02		51	.32
	16	.08		8	.02		52	.33
	17	.08		9	.03		53	.33
	18	.09		10	.03		54	.34
	19	.10		11	.04		55	.35
	20	.10		12	.04		56	.36
	21	.11		13	.05		57	.37
	22	.12		14	.06		58	.38
	23	.13		15	.06		59	.38
	24	.13		16	.07		60	.39
	25	.14		17	.08			
	26	.15		18	.08	130	5	.01
	27	.16		19	.09		6	.01
	28	.17		20	.09		7	.02
	29	.17		21	.10		8	.02

APPENDIX 1 (cont.)

LOWER 1% LIMITS FOR A BINOMIAL VARIABLE

N_c	X_c	P'_c	N_c	X_c	P'_c	N_c	X_c	P'_c
130	9	.03	130	53	.31	140	35	.17
	10	.03		54	.31		36	.17
	11	.04		55	.32		37	.18
	12	.04		56	.33		38	.19
	13	.05		57	.33		39	.19
	14	.06		58	.34		40	.20
	15	.06		59	.35		41	.21
	16	.07		60	.36		42	.21
	17	.08		61	.37		43	.22
	18	.08		62	.38		44	.23
	19	.09		63	.38		45	.23
	20	.09		64	.39		46	.24
	21	.10		65	.39		47	.24
	22	.11					48	.25
	23	.11	140	5	.01		49	.26
	24	.12		6	.01		50	.26
	25	.12		7	.01		51	.27
	26	.13		8	.02		52	.28
	27	.13		9	.02		53	.28
	28	.14		10	.03		54	.29
	29	.14		11	.03		55	.30
	30	.15		12	.04		56	.30
	31	.16		13	.04		57	.31
	32	.16		14	.05		58	.32
	33	.17		15	.05		59	.32
	34	.18		16	.06		60	.33
	35	.18		17	.06		61	.34
	36	.19		18	.07		62	.34
	37	.20		19	.07		63	.35
	38	.20		20	.08		64	.36
	39	.21		21	.08		65	.36
	40	.22		22	.09		66	.37
	41	.22		23	.10		67	.38
	42	.23		24	.10		68	.38
	43	.24		25	.11		69	.39
	44	.24		26	.11		70	.40
	45	.25		27	.12			
	46	.26		28	.13	150	6	.01
	47	.26		29	.13		7	.01
	48	.27		30	.14		8	.02
	49	.28		31	.14		9	.02
	50	.29		32	.15		10	.03
	51	.29		33	.16		11	.03
	52	.30		34	.16		12	.04

APPENDIX 1 (cont.)

LOWER 1% LIMITS FOR A BINOMIAL VARIABLE

N_c	X_c	P_c'	N_c	X_c	P_c'	N_c	X_c	P_c'
150	13	.04	150	57	.29	160	30	.12
	14	.04		58	.29		31	.13
	15	.05		59	.30		32	.13
	16	.05		60	.31		33	.14
	17	.06		61	.31		34	.14
	18	.06		62	.32		35	.15
	19	.07		63	.33		36	.15
	20	.07		64	.33		37	.16
	21	.08		65	.34		38	.16
	22	.08		66	.34		39	.17
	23	.09		67	.35		40	.17
	24	.09		68	.36		41	.18
	25	.10		69	.36		42	.19
	26	.11		70	.37		43	.19
	27	.11		71	.38		44	.20
	28	.11		72	.38		45	.20
	29	.13		73	.39		46	.21
	30	.13		74	.40		47	.21
	31	.13		75	.40		48	.22
	32	.14					49	.22
	33	.15	160	6	.01		50	.23
	34	.15		7	.01		51	.23
	35	.16		8	.02		52	.24
	36	.16		9	.02		53	.25
	37	.17		10	.02		54	.25
	38	.17		11	.03		55	.26
	39	.18		12	.03		56	.26
	40	.19		13	.04		57	.27
	41	.19		14	.04		58	.27
	42	.20		15	.05		59	.28
	43	.20		16	.05		60	.29
	44	.21		17	.06		61	.29
	45	.22		18	.06		62	.30
	46	.22		19	.06		63	.30
	47	.23		20	.07		64	.31
	48	.23		21	.07		65	.31
	49	.24		22	.08		66	.32
	50	.25		23	.08		67	.33
	51	.25		24	.09		68	.33
	52	.26		25	.09		69	.34
	53	.26		26	.10		70	.34
	54	.27		27	.10		71	.35
	55	.28		28	.11		72	.36
	56	.28		29	.11		73	.36

APPENDIX 1 (cont.)

LOWER 1% LIMITS FOR A BINOMIAL VARIABLE

N_C	X_C	P_C'	N_C	X_C	P_C'	N_C	X_C	P_C'
160	74	.37	170	42	.17	180	6	.01
	75	.38		43	.18		7	.01
	76	.38		44	.18		8	.01
	77	.39		45	.19		9	.02
	78	.39		46	.19		10	.02
	79	.40		47	.20		11	.02
	80	.41		48	.20		12	.03
				49	.21		13	.03
170	6	.01		50	.21		14	.04
	7	.01		51	.22		15	.04
	8	.01		52	.23		16	.04
	9	.02		53	.23		17	.05
	10	.02		54	.24		18	.05
	11	.03		55	.24		19	.06
	12	.03		56	.25		20	.06
	13	.03		57	.25		21	.07
	14	.04		58	.26		22	.07
	15	.04		59	.26		23	.07
	16	.05		60	.27		24	.08
	17	.05		61	.27		25	.08
	18	.06		62	.28		26	.09
	19	.06		63	.28		27	.09
	20	.06		64	.29		28	.10
	21	.07		65	.30		29	.10
	22	.07		66	.30		30	.11
	23	.08		67	.31		31	.11
	24	.08		68	.31		32	.12
	25	.09		69	.32		33	.12
	26	.09		70	.32		34	.13
	27	.10		71	.33		35	.13
	28	.10		72	.33		36	.13
	29	.11		73	.34		37	.14
	30	.11		74	.35		38	.14
	31	.12		75	.35		39	.15
	32	.13		76	.36		40	.15
	33	.13		77	.36		41	.16
	34	.13		78	.37		42	.17
	35	.14		79	.38		43	.17
	36	.14		80	.38		44	.17
	37	.15		81	.39		45	.18
	38	.15		82	.39		46	.18
	39	.16		83	.40		47	.19
	40	.16		84	.40		48	.19
	41	.17		85	.41		49	.20

APPENDIX 1 (cont.)

LOWER 1% LIMITS FOR A BINOMIAL VARIABLE

N_C	X_C	P_C'	N_C	X_C	P_C'	N_C	X_C	P_C'
180	50	.20	190	8	.01	190	52	.20
	51	.21		9	.02		53	.21
	52	.21		10	.02		54	.21
	53	.22		11	.02		55	.21
	54	.22		12	.03		56	.22
	55	.23		13	.03		57	.22
	56	.23		14	.03		58	.23
	57	.24		15	.04		59	.23
	58	.24		16	.04		60	.24
	59	.25		17	.05		61	.24
	60	.25		18	.05		62	.25
	61	.26		19	.05		63	.25
	62	.26		20	.06		64	.26
	63	.27		21	.06		65	.26
	64	.27		22	.07		66	.27
	65	.28		23	.07		67	.27
	66	.28		24	.07		68	.28
	67	.29		25	.08		69	.28
	68	.29		26	.08		70	.29
	69	.30		27	.09		71	.29
	70	.30		28	.09		72	.30
	71	.31		29	.10		73	.30
	72	.31		30	.10		74	.31
	73	.32		31	.10		75	.31
	74	.33		32	.11		76	.32
	75	.33		33	.11		77	.32
	76	.33		34	.12		78	.33
	77	.34		35	.13		79	.33
	78	.35		36	.13		80	.34
	79	.35		37	.13		81	.34
	80	.36		38	.14		82	.35
	81	.36		39	.14		83	.35
	82	.37		40	.14		84	.36
	83	.38		41	.15		85	.36
	84	.38		42	.15		86	.37
	85	.38		43	.16		87	.38
	86	.39		44	.17		88	.38
	87	.39		45	.17		89	.38
	88	.40		46	.17		90	.39
	89	.41		47	.18		91	.39
	90	.41		48	.18		92	.40
				49	.19		93	.40
190	6	.01		50	.19		94	.41
	7	.01		51	.20		95	.42

APPENDIX 1 (cont.)

LOWER 1% LIMITS FOR A BINOMIAL VARIABLE

N_c	X_c	P_c'	N_c	X_c	P_c'	N_c	X_c	P_c'
200	7	.01	200	51	.19	200	95	.39
	8	.01		52	.19		96	.40
	9	.01		53	.19		97	.40
	10	.02		54	.20		98	.41
	11	.02		55	.20		99	.41
	12	.03		56	.21		100	.42
	13	.03		57	.21			
	14	.03		58	.22			
	15	.04		59	.22			
	16	.04		60	.23			
	17	.04		61	.23			
	18	.05		62	.23			
	19	.05		63	.24			
	20	.05		64	.24			
	21	.06		65	.25			
	22	.06		66	.25			
	23	.07		67	.26			
	24	.07		68	.26			
	25	.07		69	.27			
	26	.08		70	.27			
	27	.08		71	.28			
	28	.09		72	.28			
	29	.09		73	.29			
	30	.09		74	.29			
	31	.10		75	.30			
	32	.10		76	.30			
	33	.11		77	.30			
	34	.11		78	.31			
	35	.12		79	.31			
	36	.12		80	.32			
	37	.13		81	.32			
	38	.13		82	.33			
	39	.13		83	.33			
	40	.14		84	.34			
	41	.14		85	.34			
	42	.15		86	.35			
	43	.15		87	.35			
	44	.15		88	.36			
	45	.16		89	.36			
	46	.17		90	.37			
	47	.17		91	.37			
	48	.17		92	.38			
	49	.18		93	.38			
	50	.18		94	.39			

APPENDIX 1 (cont.)

UPPER 99% LIMITS FOR A BINOMIAL VARIABLE

N_t	X_t	P_t'	N_t	X_t	P_t'	N_t	X_t	P_t'
10	0	.37	13	11	.99	16	13	.97
	1	.51					14	.99
	2	.61	14	0	.28			
	3	.70		1	.39	17	0	.24
	4	.78		2	.48		1	.33
	5	.85		3	.56		2	.41
	6	.91		4	.63		3	.48
	7	.95		5	.69		4	.54
	8	.99		6	.75		5	.60
				7	.81		6	.66
11	0	.34		8	.86		7	.71
	1	.47		9	.90		8	.76
	2	.57		10	.94		9	.80
	3	.66		11	.97		10	.85
	4	.74		12	.99		11	.88
	5	.81					12	.92
	6	.87	15	0	.26		13	.95
	7	.92		1	.37		14	.97
	8	.96		2	.45		15	.99
	9	.99		3	.53			
				4	.60	18	0	.23
12	0	.32		5	.66		1	.32
	1	.44		6	.72		2	.39
	2	.54		7	.77		3	.46
	3	.62		8	.82		4	.52
	4	.70		9	.87		5	.58
	5	.77		10	.91		6	.63
	6	.83		11	.94		7	.68
	7	.88		12	.97		8	.73
	8	.93		13	.99		9	.77
	9	.96					10	.82
	10	.99	16	0	.25		11	.86
				1	.35		12	.89
13	0	.30		2	.43		13	.92
	1	.41		3	.50		14	.95
	2	.51		4	.57		15	.98
	3	.59		5	.63		16	.99
	4	.66		6	.69			
	5	.73		7	.74	19	0	.22
	6	.79		8	.79		1	.30
	7	.84		9	.83		2	.38
	8	.89		10	.88		3	.44
	9	.93		11	.91		4	.50
	10	.97		12	.95		5	.55

APPENDIX 1 (cont.)

UPPER 99% LIMITS FOR A BINOMIAL VARIABLE

N_t	X_t	P_t'	N_t	X_t	P_t'	N_t	X_t	P_t'
19	6	.61	21	11	.78	23	12	.76
	7	.66		12	.81		13	.80
	8	.70		13	.85		14	.83
	9	.75		14	.88		15	.86
	10	.79		15	.91		16	.89
	11	.83		16	.94		17	.92
	12	.86		17	.96		18	.94
	13	.90		18	.98		19	.96
	14	.93		19	.99		20	.98
	15	.95					21	.99
	16	.98	22	0	.19			
	17	.99		1	.27	24	0	.17
				2	.33		1	.25
20	0	.21		3	.39		2	.31
	1	.29		4	.44		3	.36
	2	.36		5	.49		4	.41
	3	.42		6	.54		5	.46
	4	.48		7	.59		6	.51
	5	.53		8	.63		7	.55
	6	.58		9	.67		8	.59
	7	.63		10	.71		9	.63
	8	.68		11	.75		10	.67
	9	.72		12	.79		11	.71
	10	.76		13	.82		12	.74
	11	.80		14	.85		13	.78
	12	.84		15	.88		14	.81
	13	.87		16	.91		15	.84
	14	.90		17	.94		16	.87
	15	.93		18	.96		17	.90
	16	.96		19	.98		18	.92
	17	.98		20	.99		19	.94
	18	.99					20	.97
			23	0	.18		21	.98
21	0	.20		1	.26		22	.99
	1	.28		2	.32			
	2	.34		3	.38	25	0	.17
	3	.41		4	.43		1	.24
	4	.46		5	.48		2	.30
	5	.51		6	.52		3	.35
	6	.56		7	.57		4	.40
	7	.61		8	.61		5	.45
	8	.65		9	.65		6	.49
	9	.70		10	.69		7	.53
	10	.74		11	.73		8	.57

APPENDIX 1 (cont.)

UPPER 99% LIMITS FOR A BINOMIAL VARIABLE

N_t	X_t	P_t'	N_t	X_t	P_t'	N_t	X_t	P_t'
25	9	.61	27	3	.33	28	21	.91
	10	.65		4	.37		22	.93
	11	.68		5	.42		23	.95
	12	.72		6	.46		24	.97
	13	.75		7	.50		25	.98
	14	.79		8	.54			
	15	.82		9	.58	29	0	.15
	16	.85		10	.61		1	.21
	17	.87		11	.65		2	.26
	18	.90		12	.68		3	.31
	19	.92		13	.71		4	.35
	20	.95		14	.74		5	.39
	21	.97		15	.77		6	.43
	22	.98		16	.80		7	.47
	23	.99		17	.83		8	.51
				18	.86		9	.54
26	0	.16		19	.88		10	.58
	1	.23		20	.91		11	.61
	2	.29		21	.93		12	.64
	3	.34		22	.95		13	.68
	4	.39		23	.97		14	.71
	5	.43		24	.98		15	.74
	6	.47					16	.76
	7	.52	28	0	.15		17	.79
	8	.55		1	.22		18	.82
	9	.59		2	.27		19	.84
	10	.63		3	.32		20	.87
	11	.66		4	.36		21	.89
	12	.70		5	.40		22	.91
	13	.73		6	.45		23	.94
	14	.76		7	.48		24	.95
	15	.79		8	.52		25	.97
	16	.82		9	.56		26	.99
	17	.85		10	.59			
	18	.88		11	.63	30	0	.14
	19	.90		12	.66		1	.20
	20	.93		13	.69		2	.25
	21	.95		14	.72		3	.30
	22	.97		15	.75		4	.34
	23	.98		16	.78		5	.38
				17	.81		6	.42
27	0	.16		18	.84		7	.46
	1	.22		19	.86		8	.49
	2	.28		20	.89		9	.53

APPENDIX 1 (cont.)

UPPER 99% LIMITS FOR A BINOMIAL VARIABLE

N_t	X_t	P_t'	N_t	X_t	P_t'	N_t	X_t	P_t'
30	10	.56	31	25	.94	33	8	.46
	11	.59		26	.96		9	.49
	12	.63		27	.97		10	.52
	13	.66		28	.99		11	.55
	14	.69					12	.58
	15	.72	32	0	.13		13	.61
	16	.75		1	.19		14	.64
	17	.77		2	.24		15	.67
	18	.80		3	.28		16	.69
	19	.83		4	.32		17	.72
	20	.85		5	.36		18	.75
	21	.87		6	.40		19	.77
	22	.90		7	.43		20	.80
	23	.92		8	.47		21	.82
	24	.94		9	.50		22	.84
	25	.96		10	.53		23	.87
	26	.97		11	.56		24	.89
	27	.99		12	.60		25	.91
				13	.63		26	.93
31	0	.14		14	.65		27	.94
	1	.20		15	.68		28	.96
	2	.25		16	.71		29	.98
	3	.29		17	.74		30	.99
	4	.33		18	.76			
	5	.37		19	.79	34	0	.13
	6	.41		20	.81		1	.18
	7	.45		21	.84		2	.23
	8	.48		22	.86		3	.27
	9	.51		23	.88		4	.31
	10	.55		24	.90		5	.34
	11	.58		25	.92		6	.38
	12	.61		26	.94		7	.41
	13	.64		27	.96		8	.44
	14	.67		28	.97		9	.48
	15	.70		29	.99		10	.51
	16	.73					11	.54
	17	.75	33	0	.13		12	.57
	18	.78		1	.19		13	.60
	19	.81		2	.23		14	.62
	20	.83		3	.27		15	.65
	21	.86		4	.31		16	.68
	22	.88		5	.35		17	.70
	23	.90		6	.39		18	.73
	24	.92		7	.42		19	.76

APPENDIX 1 (cont.)

UPPER 99% LIMITS FOR A BINOMIAL VARIABLE

N_t	X_t	P_t'	N_t	X_t	P_t'	N_t	X_t	P_t'
34	20	.78	35	31	.98	37	6	.35
	21	.80		32	.99		7	.38
	22	.83					8	.41
	23	.85	36	0	.12		9	.44
	24	.87		1	.17		10	.47
	25	.89		2	.21		11	.50
	26	.91		3	.25		12	.53
	27	.93		4	.29		13	.56
	28	.95		5	.33		14	.58
	29	.96		6	.36		15	.61
	30	.98		7	.39		16	.63
	31	.99		8	.42		17	.66
				9	.45		18	.68
35	0	.12		10	.48		19	.71
	1	.18		11	.51		20	.73
	2	.22		12	.54		21	.75
	3	.26		13	.57		22	.78
	4	.30		14	.60		23	.80
	5	.33		15	.62		24	.82
	6	.37		16	.65		25	.84
	7	.40		17	.67		26	.86
	8	.43		18	.70		27	.88
	9	.46		19	.72		28	.90
	10	.50		20	.75		29	.92
	11	.52		21	.77		30	.93
	12	.55		22	.79		31	.95
	13	.58		23	.82		32	.97
	14	.61		24	.84		33	.98
	15	.64		25	.86		34	.99
	16	.66		26	.88			
	17	.69		27	.90	38	0	.11
	18	.71		28	.92		1	.16
	19	.74		29	.93		2	.20
	20	.76		30	.95		3	.24
	21	.79		31	.96		4	.28
	22	.81		32	.98		5	.31
	23	.83		33	.99		6	.34
	24	.85					7	.37
	25	.87	37	0	.12		8	.40
	26	.89		1	.17		9	.43
	27	.91		2	.21		10	.46
	28	.93		3	.25		11	.49
	29	.95		4	.28		12	.52
	30	.96		5	.32		13	.54

APPENDIX 1 (cont.)

UPPER 99% LIMITS FOR A BINOMIAL VARIABLE

N_t	X_t	P_t'	N_t	X_t	P_t'	N_t	X_t	P_t'
38	14	.57	39	21	.73	40	27	.83
	15	.60		22	.75		28	.85
	16	.62		23	.77		29	.87
	17	.65		24	.79		30	.89
	18	.67		25	.81		31	.91
	19	.69		26	.83		32	.92
	20	.72		27	.85		33	.94
	21	.74		28	.87		34	.95
	22	.76		29	.89		35	.97
	23	.78		30	.91		36	.98
	24	.81		31	.92		37	.99
	25	.83		32	.94			
	26	.85		33	.95	41	0	.11
	27	.87		34	.97		1	.15
	28	.88		35	.98		2	.19
	29	.90		36	.99		3	.23
	30	.92					4	.26
	31	.94	40	0	.11		5	.29
	32	.95		1	.16		6	.32
	33	.97		2	.20		7	.35
	34	.98		3	.23		8	.38
	35	.99		4	.26		9	.41
				5	.30		10	.43
39	0	.11		6	.33		11	.46
	1	.16		7	.36		12	.49
	2	.20		8	.39		13	.51
	3	.24		9	.41		14	.54
	4	.27		10	.44		15	.56
	5	.30		11	.47		16	.58
	6	.34		12	.50		17	.61
	7	.37		13	.52		18	.63
	8	.40		14	.55		19	.65
	9	.42		15	.57		20	.68
	10	.45		16	.60		21	.70
	11	.48		17	.62		22	.72
	12	.51		18	.64		23	.74
	13	.53		19	.67		24	.76
	14	.56		20	.69		25	.78
	15	.58		21	.71		26	.80
	16	.61		22	.73		27	.82
	17	.63		23	.75		28	.84
	18	.66		24	.78		29	.86
	19	.68		25	.80		30	.88
	20	.70		26	.82		31	.89

APPENDIX 1 (cont.)

UPPER 99% LIMITS FOR A BINOMIAL VARIABLE

N_t	X_t	P_t'	N_t	X_t	P_t'	N_t	X_t	P_t'
41	32	.91	42	36	.96	43	39	.98
	33	.93		37	.97		40	.99
	34	.94		38	.98			
	35	.96		39	.99	44	0	.10
	36	.97					1	.14
	37	.98	43	0	.10		2	.18
	38	.99		1	.15		3	.21
				2	.18		4	.24
42	0	.10		3	.22		5	.27
	1	.15		4	.25		6	.30
	2	.19		5	.28		7	.33
	3	.22		6	.31		8	.36
	4	.25		7	.34		9	.38
	5	.28		8	.36		10	.41
	6	.31		9	.39		11	.43
	7	.34		10	.42		12	.46
	8	.37		11	.44		13	.48
	9	.40		12	.47		14	.50
	10	.42		13	.49		15	.53
	11	.45		14	.51		16	.55
	12	.48		15	.54		17	.57
	13	.50		16	.56		18	.60
	14	.52		17	.58		19	.62
	15	.55		18	.61		20	.64
	16	.57		19	.63		21	.66
	17	.60		20	.65		22	.68
	18	.62		21	.67		23	.70
	19	.64		22	.69		24	.72
	20	.66		23	.71		25	.74
	21	.68		24	.73		26	.76
	22	.71		25	.75		27	.78
	23	.73		26	.77		28	.80
	24	.75		27	.79		29	.82
	25	.77		28	.81		30	.83
	26	.79		29	.83		31	.85
	27	.81		30	.85		32	.87
	28	.83		31	.87		33	.89
	29	.84		32	.88		34	.90
	30	.86		33	.90		35	.92
	31	.88		34	.91		36	.93
	32	.90		35	.93		37	.95
	33	.91		36	.94		38	.96
	34	.93		37	.96		39	.97
	35	.94		38	.97		40	.98

APPENDIX 1 (cont.)

UPPER 99% LIMITS FOR A BINOMIAL VARIABLE

N_t	X_t	P_t'	N_t	X_t	P_t'	N_t	X_t	P_t'
44	41	.99	45	42	.99	46	42	.98
							43	.99
45	0	.10	46	0	.10			
	1	.14		1	.14	47	0	.09
	2	.17		2	.17		1	.13
	3	.21		3	.20		2	.17
	4	.24		4	.23		3	.20
	5	.27		5	.26		4	.23
	6	.29		6	.29		5	.26
	7	.32		7	.32		6	.28
	8	.35		8	.34		7	.31
	9	.37		9	.37		8	.34
	10	.40		10	.39		9	.36
	11	.42		11	.42		10	.38
	12	.45		12	.44		11	.41
	13	.47		13	.46		12	.43
	14	.49		14	.49		13	.45
	15	.52		15	.51		14	.48
	16	.54		16	.53		15	.50
	17	.56		17	.55		16	.52
	18	.58		18	.57		17	.54
	19	.61		19	.60		18	.56
	20	.63		20	.62		19	.58
	21	.65		21	.64		20	.61
	22	.67		22	.66		21	.63
	23	.69		23	.68		22	.65
	24	.71		24	.70		23	.67
	25	.73		25	.72		24	.68
	26	.75		26	.73		25	.70
	27	.77		27	.75		26	.72
	28	.78		28	.77		27	.74
	29	.80		29	.79		28	.76
	30	.82		30	.81		29	.78
	31	.84		31	.83		30	.79
	32	.86		32	.84		31	.81
	33	.87		33	.86		32	.83
	34	.89		34	.87		33	.85
	35	.90		35	.89		34	.86
	36	.92		36	.91		35	.88
	37	.93		37	.92		36	.89
	38	.95		38	.93		37	.91
	39	.96		39	.95		38	.92
	40	.97		40	.96		39	.94
	41	.98		41	.97		40	.95

APPENDIX 1 (cont.)

UPPER 99% LIMITS FOR A BINOMIAL VARIABLE

N_t	X_t	P_t'	N_t	X_t	P_t'	N_t	X_t	P_t'
47	41	.96	48	39	.92	49	36	.87
	42	.97		40	.94		37	.88
	43	.98		41	.95		38	.90
	44	.99		42	.96		39	.91
				43	.97		40	.93
48	0	.09		44	.98		41	.94
	1	.13		45	.99		42	.95
	2	.16					43	.96
	3	.20	49	0	.09		44	.97
	4	.22		1	.13		45	.98
	5	.25		2	.16		46	.99
	6	.28		3	.19			
	7	.30		4	.22	50	0	.09
	8	.33		5	.25		1	.13
	9	.35		6	.27		2	.16
	10	.38		7	.30		3	.19
	11	.40		8	.32		4	.22
	12	.42		9	.35		5	.24
	13	.45		10	.37		6	.27
	14	.47		11	.39		7	.29
	15	.49		12	.42		8	.32
	16	.51		13	.44		9	.34
	17	.53		14	.46		10	.36
	18	.55		15	.48		11	.39
	19	.57		16	.50		12	.41
	20	.59		17	.52		13	.43
	21	.61		18	.54		14	.45
	22	.63		19	.56		15	.47
	23	.65		20	.58		16	.49
	24	.67		21	.60		17	.51
	25	.69		22	.62		18	.53
	26	.71		23	.64		19	.55
	27	.73		24	.66		20	.57
	28	.75		25	.68		21	.59
	29	.76		26	.70		22	.61
	30	.78		27	.72		23	.63
	31	.80		28	.74		24	.65
	32	.82		29	.75		25	.67
	33	.83		30	.77		26	.69
	34	.85		31	.79		27	.71
	35	.87		32	.80		28	.72
	36	.88		33	.82		29	.74
	37	.90		34	.84		30	.76
	38	.91		35	.85		31	.78

APPENDIX 1 (cont.)

UPPER 99% LIMITS FOR A BINOMIAL VARIABLE

N_t	X_t	P_t'	N_t	X_t	P_t'	N_t	X_t	P_t'
50	32	.79	51	27	.69	52	21	.57
	33	.81		28	.71		22	.59
	34	.82		29	.73		23	.61
	35	.84		30	.75		24	.63
	36	.86		31	.76		25	.65
	37	.87		32	.78		26	.67
	38	.89		33	.80		27	.68
	39	.90		34	.81		28	.70
	40	.91		35	.83		29	.72
	41	.93		36	.84		30	.74
	42	.94		37	.86		31	.75
	43	.95		38	.87		32	.77
	44	.96		39	.89		33	.78
	45	.97		40	.90		34	.80
	46	.98		41	.92		35	.82
	47	.99		42	.93		36	.83
				43	.94		37	.85
51	0	.09		44	.95		38	.86
	1	.12		45	.96		39	.88
	2	.16		46	.98		40	.89
	3	.18		47	.98		41	.90
	4	.21		48	.99		42	.92
	5	.24					43	.93
	6	.26	52	0	.08		44	.94
	7	.29		1	.12		45	.95
	8	.31		2	.15		46	.97
	9	.33		3	.18		47	.98
	10	.36		4	.21		48	.98
	11	.38		5	.23		49	.99
	12	.40		6	.26			
	13	.42		7	.28	53	0	.08
	14	.44		8	.31		1	.12
	15	.47		9	.33		2	.15
	16	.49		10	.35		3	.18
	17	.51		11	.37		4	.20
	18	.53		12	.39		5	.23
	19	.55		13	.42		6	.25
	20	.57		14	.44		7	.28
	21	.58		15	.46		8	.30
	22	.60		16	.48		9	.32
	23	.62		17	.50		10	.35
	24	.64		18	.52		11	.37
	25	.66		19	.54		12	.39
	26	.68		20	.56		13	.41

APPENDIX 1 (cont.)

UPPER 99% LIMITS FOR A BINOMIAL VARIABLE

N_t	X_t	P_t'	N_t	X_t	P_t'	N_t	X_t	P_t'
53	14	.43	54	7	.27	56	0	.08
	15	.45		8	.30		1	.11
	16	.47		9	.32		2	.14
	17	.49		10	.34		3	.17
	18	.51		11	.36		4	.19
	19	.53		12	.38		5	.22
	20	.55		13	.40		6	.24
	21	.57		14	.42		7	.26
	22	.58		15	.44		8	.29
	23	.60		16	.46		9	.31
	24	.62		17	.48		10	.33
	25	.64		18	.50		11	.35
	26	.66		19	.52		12	.37
	27	.67		20	.54		13	.39
	28	.69		21	.56		14	.41
	29	.71		22	.58		15	.43
	30	.72		23	.59		16	.45
	31	.74		24	.61		17	.47
	32	.76		25	.63		18	.49
	33	.77		26	.65		19	.50
	34	.79		27	.66		20	.52
	35	.80		28	.68		21	.54
	36	.82		29	.70		22	.56
	37	.84		30	.71		23	.58
	38	.85		31	.73		24	.59
	39	.86		32	.75		25	.61
	40	.88		33	.76		26	.63
	41	.89		34	.78		27	.64
	42	.91		35	.79		28	.66
	43	.92		36	.81		29	.68
	44	.93		37	.82		30	.69
	45	.94		38	.84		31	.71
	46	.96		39	.85		32	.73
	47	.97		40	.87		33	.74
	48	.98		41	.88		34	.76
	49	.99		42	.89		35	.77
				43	.91		36	.79
54	0	.08		44	.92		37	.80
	1	.12		45	.93		38	.82
	2	.15		46	.95		39	.83
	3	.18		47	.96		40	.84
	4	.20		48	.97		41	.86
	5	.23		49	.98		42	.87
	6	.25		50	.99		43	.89

APPENDIX 1 (cont.)

UPPER 99% LIMITS FOR A BINOMIAL VARIABLE

N_t	X_t	P_t'	N_t	X_t	P_t'	N_t	X_t	P_t'
56	44	.90	58	33	.72	60	20	.49
	45	.91		34	.74		21	.51
	46	.92		35	.75		22	.53
	47	.94		36	.77		23	.54
	48	.95		37	.78		24	.56
	49	.96		38	.79		25	.58
	50	.97		39	.81		26	.59
	51	.98		40	.82		27	.61
	52	.99		41	.84		28	.62
	53	.99		42	.85		29	.64
				43	.86		30	.66
58	0	.08		44	.88		31	.67
	1	.11		45	.89		32	.69
	2	.14		46	.90		33	.70
	3	.16		47	.91		34	.72
	4	.19		48	.93		35	.73
	5	.21		49	.94		36	.75
	6	.23		50	.95		37	.76
	7	.26		51	.96		38	.77
	8	.28		52	.97		39	.79
	9	.30		53	.98		40	.80
	10	.32		54	.99		41	.82
	11	.34		55	.99		42	.83
	12	.36					43	.84
	13	.38	60	0	.07		44	.86
	14	.40		1	.11		45	.87
	15	.42		2	.13		46	.88
	16	.43		3	.16		47	.89
	17	.45		4	.18		48	.91
	18	.47		5	.21		49	.92
	19	.49		6	.23		50	.93
	20	.51		7	.25		51	.94
	21	.52		8	.27		52	.95
	22	.54		9	.29		53	.96
	23	.56		10	.31		54	.97
	24	.58		11	.33		55	.98
	25	.59		12	.35		56	.99
	26	.61		13	.37		57	.99
	27	.63		14	.38			
	28	.64		15	.40	62	0	.07
	29	.66		16	.42		1	.10
	30	.67		17	.44		2	.13
	31	.69		18	.46		3	.15
	32	.70		19	.47		4	.18

APPENDIX 1 (cont.)

UPPER 99% LIMITS FOR A BINOMIAL VARIABLE

N_t	X_t	P_t'	N_t	X_t	P_t'	N_t	X_t	P_t'
62	5	.20	62	49	.90	70	0	.06
	6	.22		50	.91		2	.12
	7	.24		51	.92		4	.16
	8	.26		52	.93		6	.20
	9	.28		53	.94		8	.23
	10	.30		54	.95		10	.27
	11	.32		55	.96		12	.30
	12	.34		56	.97		14	.33
	13	.36		57	.98		16	.37
	14	.37		58	.99		18	.40
	15	.39		59	.99		20	.43
	16	.41					22	.46
	17	.43	66	0	.07		24	.49
	18	.44		2	.12		26	.52
	19	.46		4	.17		28	.55
	20	.48		6	.21		30	.58
	21	.49		8	.25		32	.60
	22	.51		10	.28		34	.63
	23	.53		12	.32		36	.66
	24	.54		14	.35		38	.68
	25	.56		16	.39		40	.71
	26	.58		18	.42		42	.74
	27	.59		20	.45		44	.76
	28	.61		22	.48		46	.78
	29	.62		24	.51		48	.81
	30	.64		26	.55		50	.83
	31	.66		28	.58		52	.86
	32	.67		30	.60		54	.88
	33	.68		32	.63		56	.90
	34	.70		34	.66		58	.92
	35	.71		36	.69		60	.94
	36	.73		38	.72		62	.96
	37	.74		40	.74		64	.97
	38	.75		42	.77		66	.99
	39	.77		44	.80			
	40	.78		46	.82	74	0	.06
	41	.80		48	.85		2	.11
	42	.81		50	.87		4	.15
	43	.82		52	.89		6	.19
	44	.84		54	.91		8	.22
	45	.85		56	.94		10	.25
	46	.86		58	.96		12	.29
	47	.87		60	.97		14	.32
	48	.89		62	.99		16	.35

APPENDIX 1 (cont.)

UPPER 99% LIMITS FOR A BINOMIAL VARIABLE

N_t	X_t	P_t'	N_t	X_t	P_t'	N_t	X_t	P_t'
74	18	.38	78	32	.55	82	42	.64
	20	.41		34	.57		44	.67
	22	.44		36	.60		46	.69
	24	.47		38	.62		48	.71
	26	.49		40	.65		50	.73
	28	.52		42	.67		52	.76
	30	.55		44	.70		54	.78
	32	.57		46	.72		56	.80
	34	.60		48	.74		58	.82
	36	.63		50	.76		60	.84
	38	.65		52	.79		62	.86
	40	.68		54	.81		64	.88
	42	.70		56	.83		66	.90
	44	.73		58	.85		68	.91
	46	.75		60	.87		70	.93
	48	.77		62	.89		72	.95
	50	.80		64	.91		74	.96
	52	.82		66	.93		76	.98
	54	.84		68	.95		78	.99
	56	.86		70	.96			
	58	.88		72	.98	86	0	.05
	60	.91		74	.99		2	.10
	62	.92					4	.13
	64	.94	82	0	.05		6	.16
	66	.96		2	.10		8	.19
	68	.98		4	.14		10	.22
	70	.99		6	.17		12	.25
				8	.20		14	.28
78	0	.06		10	.23		16	.30
	2	.10		12	.26		18	.33
	4	.14		14	.29		20	.36
	6	.18		16	.32		22	.38
	8	.21		18	.35		24	.41
	10	.24		20	.37		26	.43
	12	.27		22	.40		28	.46
	14	.30		24	.42		30	.48
	16	.33		26	.45		32	.50
	18	.36		28	.48		34	.53
	20	.39		30	.50		36	.55
	22	.42		32	.53		38	.57
	24	.44		34	.55		40	.60
	26	.47		36	.57		42	.62
	28	.50		38	.60		44	.64
	30	.52		40	.62		46	.66

APPENDIX 1 (cont.)

UPPER 99% LIMITS FOR A BINOMIAL VARIABLE

N_t	X_t	P_t'	N_t	X_t	P_t'	N_t	X_t	P_t'
86	48	.68	90	50	.68	95	48	.63
	50	.71		52	.70		50	.65
	52	.73		54	.72		52	.67
	54	.75		56	.74		54	.69
	56	.77		58	.76		56	.71
	58	.79		60	.78		58	.73
	60	.81		62	.80		60	.75
	62	.83		64	.82		62	.76
	64	.85		66	.84		64	.78
	66	.87		68	.85		66	.80
	68	.88		70	.87		68	.82
	70	.90		72	.89		70	.84
	72	.92		74	.91		72	.85
	74	.94		76	.92		74	.87
	76	.95		78	.94		76	.89
	78	.97		80	.95		78	.90
	80	.98		82	.97		80	.92
	82	.99		84	.98		82	.93
				86	.99		84	.95
90	0	.05					86	.96
	2	.09	95	0	.05		88	.98
	4	.12		2	.09		90	.99
	6	.16		4	.12			
	8	.18		6	.15	100	0	.05
	10	.21		8	.18		2	.08
	12	.24		10	.20		4	.11
	14	.27		12	.23		6	.14
	16	.29		14	.25		8	.17
	18	.32		16	.28		10	.19
	20	.34		18	.30		12	.22
	22	.37		20	.33		14	.24
	24	.39		22	.35		16	.26
	26	.41		24	.37		18	.29
	28	.44		26	.39		20	.31
	30	.46		28	.42		22	.33
	32	.48		30	.44		24	.35
	34	.51		32	.46		26	.38
	36	.53		34	.48		28	.40
	38	.55		36	.50		30	.42
	40	.57		38	.53		32	.44
	42	.59		40	.55		34	.46
	44	.62		42	.57		36	.48
	46	.64		44	.59		38	.50
	48	.66		46	.61		40	.52

APPENDIX 1 (cont.)

UPPER 99% LIMITS FOR A BINOMIAL VARIABLE

N_t	X_t	P_t'	N_t	X_t	P_t'	N_t	X_t	P_t'
100	42	.54	110	30	.38	120	8	.14
	44	.56		32	.40		10	.16
	46	.58		34	.42		12	.18
	48	.60		36	.44		14	.20
	50	.62		38	.46		16	.22
	52	.64		40	.48		18	.24
	54	.66		42	.50		20	.26
	56	.68		44	.52		22	.28
	58	.70		46	.53		24	.30
	60	.71		48	.55		26	.32
	62	.73		50	.57		28	.34
	64	.75		52	.59		30	.35
	66	.77		54	.61		32	.37
	68	.79		56	.62		34	.39
	70	.80		58	.64		36	.41
	72	.82		60	.66		38	.43
	74	.84		62	.68		40	.44
	76	.85		64	.69		42	.46
	78	.87		66	.71		44	.48
	80	.89		68	.73		46	.49
	82	.90		70	.74		48	.51
	84	.92		72	.76		50	.53
	86	.93		74	.77		52	.54
	88	.95		76	.79		54	.56
	90	.96		78	.81		56	.58
	92	.97		80	.82		58	.59
	94	.98		82	.84		60	.61
	96	.99		84	.85		62	.63
				86	.87		64	.64
110	0	.04		88	.88		66	.66
	2	.08		90	.90		68	.67
	4	.10		92	.91		70	.69
	6	.13		94	.92		72	.70
	8	.15		96	.94		74	.72
	10	.18		98	.95		76	.73
	12	.20		100	.96		78	.75
	14	.22		102	.97		80	.76
	16	.24		104	.98		82	.78
	18	.26		106	.99		84	.79
	20	.28					86	.81
	22	.30	120	0	.04		88	.82
	24	.32		2	.07		90	.84
	26	.34		4	.09		92	.85
	28	.36		6	.12		94	.87

APPENDIX 1 (cont.)

UPPER 99% LIMITS FOR A BINOMIAL VARIABLE

N_t	X_t	P_t'	N_t	X_t	P_t'	N_t	X_t	P_t'
120	96	.88	130	64	.60	140	22	.24
	98	.89		66	.61		24	.26
	100	.91		68	.63		26	.28
	102	.92		70	.64		28	.29
	104	.93		72	.66		30	.31
	106	.94		74	.67		32	.32
	108	.95		76	.69		34	.34
	110	.97		78	.70		36	.35
	112	.98		80	.71		38	.37
	114	.99		82	.73		40	.38
	116	.99		84	.74		42	.40
				86	.76		44	.41
130	0	.03		88	.77		46	.43
	2	.06		90	.78		48	.44
	4	.09		92	.80		50	.46
	6	.11		94	.81		52	.47
	8	.13		96	.82		54	.49
	10	.15		98	.84		56	.50
	12	.17		100	.85		58	.52
	14	.19		102	.86		60	.53
	16	.21		104	.88		62	.55
	18	.22		106	.89		64	.56
	20	.24		108	.90		66	.57
	22	.26		110	.91		68	.59
	24	.28		112	.92		70	.60
	26	.30		114	.94		72	.62
	28	.31		116	.95		74	.63
	30	.33		118	.96		76	.64
	32	.35		120	.97		78	.66
	34	.36		122	.98		80	.67
	36	.38		124	.99		82	.68
	38	.40		126	.99		84	.70
	40	.41					86	.71
	42	.43	140	0	.03		88	.72
	44	.44		2	.06		90	.74
	46	.46		4	.08		92	.75
	48	.48		6	.10		94	.76
	50	.49		8	.12		96	.78
	52	.51		10	.14		98	.79
	54	.52		12	.16		100	.80
	56	.54		14	.18		102	.81
	58	.55		16	.19		104	.83
	60	.57		18	.21		106	.84
	62	.58		20	.23		108	.85

APPENDIX 1 (cont.)

UPPER 99% LIMITS FOR A BINOMIAL VARIABLE

N_t	X_t	P_t'	N_t	X_t	P_t'	N_t	X_t	P_t'
140	110	.86	150	60	.50	160	0	.03
	112	.87		62	.51		2	.05
	114	.89		64	.53		4	.07
	116	.90		66	.54		6	.09
	118	.91		68	.55		8	.11
	120	.92		70	.57		10	.12
	122	.93		72	.58		12	.14
	124	.94		74	.59		14	.15
	126	.95		76	.60		16	.17
	128	.96		78	.62		18	.18
	130	.97		80	.63		20	.20
	132	.98		82	.64		22	.21
	134	.99		84	.66		24	.23
				86	.67		26	.24
150	0	.03		88	.68		28	.26
	2	.06		90	.69		30	.27
	4	.08		92	.71		32	.28
	6	.10		94	.72		34	.30
	8	.11		96	.73		36	.31
	10	.13		98	.74		38	.33
	12	.15		100	.76		40	.34
	14	.16		102	.77		42	.35
	16	.18		104	.78		44	.37
	18	.20		106	.79		46	.38
	20	.21		108	.80		48	.39
	22	.23		110	.81		50	.41
	24	.24		112	.83		52	.42
	26	.26		114	.84		54	.43
	28	.27		116	.85		56	.44
	30	.29		118	.86		58	.46
	32	.30		120	.87		60	.47
	34	.32		122	.88		62	.48
	36	.33		124	.89		64	.50
	38	.35		126	.90		66	.51
	40	.36		128	.91		68	.52
	42	.37		130	.93		70	.53
	44	.39		132	.94		72	.55
	46	.40		134	.95		74	.56
	48	.42		136	.95		76	.57
	50	.43		138	.96		78	.58
	52	.44		140	.97		80	.60
	54	.46		142	.98		82	.61
	56	.47		144	.99		84	.62
	58	.49					86	.63

APPENDIX 1 (cont.)

UPPER 99% LIMITS FOR A BINOMIAL VARIABLE

N_t	X_t	P_t'	N_t	X_t	P_t'	N_t	X_t	P_t'
160	88	.64	170	18	.17	170	106	.71
	90	.66		20	.19		108	.72
	92	.67		22	.20		110	.73
	94	.68		24	.22		112	.74
	96	.69		26	.23		114	.75
	98	.70		28	.24		116	.76
	100	.71		30	.26		118	.77
	102	.73		32	.27		120	.79
	104	.74		34	.28		122	.80
	106	.75		36	.29		124	.81
	108	.76		38	.31		126	.82
	110	.77		40	.32		128	.83
	112	.78		42	.33		130	.84
	114	.79		44	.35		132	.85
	116	.80		46	.36		134	.86
	118	.82		48	.37		136	.87
	120	.83		50	.38		138	.88
	122	.84		52	.40		140	.89
	124	.85		54	.41		142	.90
	126	.86		56	.42		144	.91
	128	.87		58	.43		146	.92
	130	.88		60	.44		148	.93
	132	.89		62	.46		150	.93
	134	.90		64	.47		152	.94
	136	.91		66	.48		154	.95
	138	.92		68	.49		156	.96
	140	.93		70	.50		158	.97
	142	.94		72	.52		160	.98
	144	.95		74	.53		162	.98
	146	.96		76	.54		164	.99
	148	.97		78	.55			
	150	.97		80	.56	180	0	.03
	152	.98		82	.57		2	.05
	154	.99		84	.59		4	.06
				86	.60		6	.08
170	0	.03		88	.61		8	.10
	2	.05		90	.62		10	.11
	4	.07		92	.63		12	.12
	6	.08		94	.64		14	.14
	8	.10		96	.65		16	.15
	10	.12		98	.67		18	.16
	12	.13		100	.68		20	.18
	14	.15		102	.69		22	.19
	16	.16		104	.70		24	.20

APPENDIX 1 (cont.)

UPPER 99% LIMITS FOR A BINOMIAL VARIABLE

N_t	X_t	P_t'	N_t	X_t	P_t'	N_t	X_t	P_t'
180	26	.22	180	114	.72	190	24	.19
	28	.23		116	.73		26	.21
	30	.24		118	.74		28	.22
	32	.25		120	.75		30	.23
	34	.27		122	.76		32	.24
	36	.28		124	.77		34	.25
	38	.29		126	.78		36	.27
	40	.30		128	.79		38	.28
	42	.32		130	.80		40	.29
	44	.33		132	.81		42	.30
	46	.34		134	.82		44	.31
	48	.35		136	.83		46	.32
	50	.36		138	.84		48	.33
	52	.38		140	.85		50	.35
	54	.39		142	.86		52	.36
	56	.40		144	.87		54	.37
	58	.41		146	.88		56	.38
	60	.42		148	.88		58	.39
	62	.43		150	.89		60	.40
	64	.44		152	.90		62	.41
	66	.46		154	.91		64	.42
	68	.47		156	.92		66	.43
	70	.48		158	.93		68	.44
	72	.49		160	.94		70	.46
	74	.50		162	.95		72	.47
	76	.51		164	.95		74	.48
	78	.52		166	.96		76	.49
	80	.53		168	.97		78	.50
	82	.55		170	.98		80	.51
	84	.56		172	.98		82	.52
	86	.57		174	.99		84	.53
	88	.58					86	.54
	90	.59	190	0	.02		88	.55
	92	.60		2	.04		90	.56
	94	.61		4	.06		92	.57
	96	.62		6	.08		94	.58
	98	.63		8	.09		96	.59
	100	.64		10	.10		98	.60
	102	.65		12	.12		100	.61
	104	.66		14	.13		102	.62
	106	.68		16	.14		104	.63
	108	.69		18	.16		106	.64
	110	.70		20	.17		108	.65
	112	.71		22	.18		110	.66

APPENDIX 1 (cont.)

UPPER 99% LIMITS FOR A BINOMIAL VARIABLE

N_t	X_t	P_t'	N_t	X_t	P_t'	N_t	X_t	P_t'
190	112	.67	200	12	.11	200	100	.59
	114	.68		14	.12		102	.59
	116	.69		16	.14		104	.60
	118	.70		18	.15		106	.61
	120	.71		20	.16		108	.62
	122	.72		22	.17		110	.63
	124	.73		24	.18		112	.64
	126	.74		26	.20		114	.65
	128	.75		28	.21		116	.66
	130	.76		30	.22		118	.67
	132	.77		32	.23		120	.68
	134	.78		34	.24		122	.69
	136	.79		36	.25		124	.70
	138	.80		38	.26		126	.71
	140	.81		40	.28		128	.72
	142	.82		42	.29		130	.73
	144	.83		44	.30		132	.74
	146	.84		46	.31		134	.75
	148	.85		48	.32		136	.76
	150	.86		50	.33		138	.77
	152	.86		52	.34		140	.77
	154	.87		54	.35		142	.78
	156	.88		56	.36		144	.79
	158	.89		58	.37		146	.80
	160	.90		60	.38		148	.81
	162	.91		62	.39		150	.82
	164	.92		64	.40		152	.83
	166	.93		66	.41		154	.84
	168	.93		68	.42		156	.85
	170	.94		70	.43		158	.85
	172	.95		72	.44		160	.86
	174	.96		74	.45		162	.87
	176	.96		76	.47		164	.88
	178	.97		78	.48		166	.89
	180	.98		80	.49		168	.90
	182	.99		82	.50		170	.90
	184	.99		84	.51		172	.91
				86	.52		174	.92
200	0	.02		88	.53		176	.93
	2	.04		90	.54		178	.94
	4	.06		92	.55		180	.94
	6	.07		94	.56		182	.95
	8	.09		96	.57		184	.96
	10	.10		98	.58		186	.97

APPENDIX 1 (cont.)

UPPER 99% LIMITS FOR A BINOMIAL VARIABLE

N_t	X_t	P_t'
200	188	.97
	190	.98
	192	.99
	194	.99

APPENDIX 2

Glossary of Terms,
Abbreviations, and Acronyms

Acceptable number of cases refers to a certain number of cases which are deemed by society to be acceptable

Acceptable risk refers to a risk level which is deemed by society to be acceptable.

Dose refers to that amount of a toxicant taken in by animals or humans during the course of a real or hypothetical exposure.

Experimental dose range refers to that range of doses derived from animal and epidemiological studies.

Experimental group refers to animals or humans whose exposure to a toxicant and any sequelae have been documented in a published report.

Involuntary risks are those which impinge on an individual without his or her awareness or consent.

Latent period is the time between the initial induction of a health effect and the manifestation (or detection) of the health effect. It is crudely estimated as the time (or some fraction of the time) from first exposure to the detection of the latent effect.

Life expectancy is the number of years remaining for a certain attained age. For example, the life expectancy at age 62 is 18 years.

Lifetime risk refers to a risk which results from lifetime exposure.

Linear model refers to that dose-response extrapolation model defined by the lowest biologically or statistically significant experimental dose-response point and the origin (at zero dose and zero response) used for nonthreshold (zero threshold) toxicants.

Nonthreshold (or zero threshold) toxicant refers to a substance which is known or assumed to incur some risk of adverse response at any dose above zero.

Observation time is the time from first and/or last exposure in an experimental study.

Remaining lifetime is the number of years remaining in a standard lifetime. For example, the remaining lifetime at age 60 is 14 years for a standard lifetime of 74 years.

Risk assessment refers to the characterization of the types of health effects expected from exposure to a toxicant, estimation of the probability (risk) of occurrence of adverse effects, estimation of the number of cases, and a suggested acceptable concentration of a contaminant in air, water, or food.

Risk factor refers to the excess risk per unit of dose at a specified dose level.

Risk group refers to a real or hypothetical exposure group composed of the general population and/or workers.

Safety factor method refers to that method used for calculating acceptable concentrations for threshold (nonzero threshold) toxicants.

Subexperimental dose range refers to that range of doses which is below the range derived from animal and epidemiological studies.

Threshold (or nonzero threshold) toxicant refers to a substance which is known or assumed to have no adverse effects below a certain dose.

Toxicant refers to any synthetic or natural chemical with an ability to produce adverse health effects.

Voluntary risks are those which an individual has consciously decided to accept.

ACGIH = American Conference of Governmental Industrial Hygienists

C = concentration in mg per unit of contaminated media (air, water, or food) for a certain risk group

C_j = concentration in mg per unit of contaminated media (air, water, or food) derived from an animal ($j = 1$) or human ($j = 2$) study

D_j = human dose (in mg) derived from an animal $(j = 1)$ or human $(j = 2)$ study

D_3 = dose (in mg) for an individual at risk

D_4 = risk group dose (in mg)

E = life expectancy (in years) of the youngest person in a risk group (Table 5.2)

E' = remaining lifetime from last exposure (in years)

E_j = lifetime (in years) for animals $(j = 1)$ or humans $(j = 2)$ derived from Table 4.1 or a certain study

EC = number of excess cases in a risk group

EPA = U.S. Environmental Protection Agency

Exp = expected number of cases in the exposed group of an epidemiology study

FDA = U.S. Food and Drug Administration

F_i = one of six possible safety (uncertainty) factors

$$\prod_{i=1}^{n} F_i = F_1 \cdot F_2 \cdot F_3 \cdots F_n$$

$f(D_3), f(D_4)$ = mathematical functions of dose (in mg) used to fit experimental dose-response data

I = intake in units of contaminated media (air, water, or food) per day for a certain risk group derived from Tables 4.1–4.3

I_j = intake in units of contaminated media (air, water, or food) per day derived from an animal $(j = 1)$ or human $(j = 2)$ study or from Tables 4.1–4.3

In = incidence or mortality rate for a selected cancer and year (may also be sex and race specific)

L = median human latent period (in years) for a latent response

L' = minimum human latent period (in years) for a latent response

L_j = median latent period (in years) for a latent response derived from an animal $(j = 1)$ or human $(j = 2)$ study

LD_{50} (mg/kg body weight) = median lethal dose, i.e., the single dose required to kill 50% of an animal group

LOAEL (mg/kg body weight/day) = *lowest*-observed-adverse-effect level. LOAEL refers to that dose rate of chemical at which there *are* statistically or biologically significant increases in frequency or severity of *adverse effects* between the exposed and control groups.

$LOAEL_a$ = LOAEL adjusted by dividing by one or more safety factors

N = number of subjects at risk in a risk group or experimental group

N_c = number of subjects at risk in a control group

NOAEL (mg/kg body weight/day) = *no*-observed-adverse-effect level. NOAEL refers to that dose rate of chemical at which there *are no* statistically or biologically significant increases in frequency or severity of *adverse effects* between the exposed and control groups. Statistically significant effects are observed at this level, but they are not considered to be adverse.

$NOAEL_a$ = NOAEL adjusted by dividing by one or more safety factors

NOEL (mg/kg body weight/day) = *no*-observed-effect level. NOEL refers to that dose rate of chemical at which there *are no* statistically or biologically significant increases in frequency or severity of *effects* between the exposed and control groups.

$NOEL_a$ = NOEL adjusted by dividing by one or more safety factors

NRC = U.S. Nuclear Regulatory Commission

N_t = number of subjects at risk in the exposed group

Obs = number of cases observed in the exposed group of an epidemiology study

OSHA = U.S. Occupational Safety and Health Administration

P = individual or group excess risk at a certain dose group

P_c = proportion responding adversely in the control group or proportion expected to respond adversely in the test group

P'_c = lower limit of control group response

P_e = control-adjusted test group response = excess risk due to the test-dose alone

P'_e = upper limit of control-adjusted test group response

PEL = permissible exposure limits established and enforced by OSHA

P_t = proportion responding adversely in the test group

P'_t = upper limit of test group response

R = ratio of the control-adjusted test group response to the human dose derived from an animal or human study (R is in units of mg^{-1})

R' = upper limit on R (in mg^{-1})

RR = relative risk = ratio of the incidence of cases in the test group to that of the control group in an epidemiology study

SMR = standard mortality ratio = ratio of observed to expected number of cases in an epidemiology study

$T = T_i$ = actual exposure time (in days or years) for a risk group or individual at risk

T_j = group exposure time (in years) derived from an animal ($j = 1$) or human ($j = 2$) study. T_j may include adjustments for latency, remaining lifetime from last exposure, and observation time from last exposure.

TLV = threshold limit values recommended by the American Conference of Governmental Industrial Hygienists (ACGIH)

T_3 = individual exposure time (in days) adjusted, if necessary, for latency and remaining lifetime from last exposure

W_j = adult body weight (in kg) derived from an animal ($j = 1$) or human ($j = 2$) study or Table 4.1

X_c = number of subjects responding adversely in the control group

X_t = number of subjects responding adversely in the test group

APPENDIX 3

Equations

4.1 $(\text{NOEL, NOAEL, or LOAEL}) = C_j \cdot I_j / W_j$

4.2 $(\text{NOEL}_a, \text{NOAEL}_a, \text{ or LOAEL}_a) = (\text{NOEL, NOAEL, or LOAEL}) / \prod\limits_{i=1}^{n} F_i$

4.3 $D_j = \dfrac{C_j \cdot I_j}{W_j \prod\limits_{i=1}^{n} F_i} \cdot 70 \cdot \dfrac{T_j}{E_j - L_j} \cdot (74 - L) \cdot 365$

4.4 $D_1 = \dfrac{C_1 \cdot I_1}{W_1 \prod\limits_{i=1}^{6} F_i} \cdot 70 \cdot \dfrac{T_1}{E_1 - L_1} \cdot (74 - L) \cdot 365$

4.5 $D_2 = \dfrac{C_2 \cdot I_2}{\prod\limits_{i=1}^{5} F_i} \cdot T_2 \cdot 365$

4.6 $P_t = X_t / N_t$

4.7 $P_c = X_c / N_c$

4.8 $P_t = \text{Obs} / N_t$

4.9 $P_c = Exp/N_t$

4.10 $RR = P_t/P_c$

4.11 $SMR = Obs/Exp$

4.12 $RR = SMR = Obs/Exp = P_t/P_c$

4.13 $P_t = RR \cdot P_c$

4.14 $P_t = SMR \cdot P_c$

4.15 $P_t = Obs \cdot P_c/Exp$

4.16 $P_c = In \cdot E$

4.17 $z = (P_t - P_c)/\{pq\ [(1/N_t) + (1/N_c)]\}^{1/2}$

4.18 $P_e = P_t - P_c$

4.19 $P_e = (P_t - P_c)/(1 - P_c)$

4.20 $P_e = (P_t - P_c)/(1 - a\ P_c)$

4.21 $P'_e = (P'_t - P'_c)/(1 - P'_c)$

4.22 $P'_t = P_t + z\ (P_t Q_t/N_t)^{1/2}$

4.23 $P'_c = P_c - z\ (P_c Q_c/N_c)^{1/2}$

4.24 $P'_e = (P'_t - P_c)/(1 - P_c)$

5.1 $P = f(D_3)$

5.2 $D_3 = C \cdot I \cdot T_3$

5.3 $P = R \cdot D_3 = R \cdot C \cdot I \cdot T_3$

5.4 $R = P_e/D_j$

5.5 $R' = P'_e/D_j$

5.6 $EC = P \cdot N = f(D_4) \cdot N$

5.7 $D_4 = C \cdot I \cdot T$

5.8 $EC = P \cdot N = R \cdot D_4 \cdot N = R \cdot C \cdot I \cdot T \cdot N$

5.9 $EC = R \cdot I \sum_{i=1}^{k} C_i\, T_i\, N_i$

5.10 $$EC = R \cdot I \cdot N \sum_{i=1}^{k} C_i T_i$$

5.11 $$EC = R \cdot I \cdot C \sum_{i=1}^{k} N_i T_i$$

5.12 $$EC = R \cdot I \cdot T \sum_{i=1}^{k} N_i C_i$$

5.13 $$EC/year = EC/(E' + T - L')$$

6.1 $$C = 1.4 \cdot 10^{-10}/[R \cdot (74 - L)]$$

6.2 $$C = 4.9 \cdot 10^{-7}/(R \cdot T_3)$$

6.3 $$C = 1.1 \cdot 10^{-9}/[R \cdot (74 - L)]$$

6.4 $$C = 1.8 \cdot 10^{-9}/[R \cdot (74 - L)]$$

6.5 $$C = D_j/(I \cdot T)$$

6.6 $$C = 1.9 \cdot 10^{-6} \cdot D_j$$

6.7 $$C = 3.9 \cdot 10^{-6} \cdot D_j$$

6.8 $$C = 1.5 \cdot 10^{-5} \cdot D_j$$

6.9 $$C = 2.5 \cdot 10^{-5} \cdot D_j$$

APPENDIX 4

U.S. FDA Risk Analysis Method for Carcinogens

The following FDA position was excerpted from "Sponsored Compounds in Food-Producing Animals; Criteria and Procedures for Evaluating the Safety of Carcinogenic Residues" *Federal Register* 50:45530–45556, 1985.

Experiments designed to observe responses in the range of interest (that is, 1 in 1 million) would require impossibly large populations of test animals. Therefore, some method is required to extrapolate data from the standard bioassays, which use much smaller and more manageable numbers of animals, to the range of interest. Because the mechanism of chemical carcinogenesis is not sufficiently understood, none of the available statistical extrapolation procedures has a fully adequate biological rationale. Matters are further complicated by the fact that the dose-response relations assumed by the various procedures diverge substantially in the projections of risks presented in the range below the lowest dose tested.

FDA's objective has been to select an extrapolation procedure that is reasonably well supported by current science and a level of risk that is protective of the public health. FDA still believes that its objectives are best met by a nonthreshold, linear-at-low-dose extrapolation procedure that determines the upper limit of the risk. After considering the comments on the 1979 proposal and other available information on extrapolation procedures, FDA has concluded that the linear interpolation procedure of Gaylor and Kodell should be adopted for these proposed regulations (Gaylor, D. W., and R. L. Kodell, "Linear Interpolation

Algorithm for Low Dose Risk Assessment of Toxic Substances," Journal of Environmental Pathology and Toxicology, 4:305–312, 1980.) As discussed in this paper, the linear interpolation procedure consists of the following steps:

1. Use any appropriate mathematical model which adequately fits the data to approximate the dose response relationship in the experimental data range.
2. Obtain the upper confidence limits on the excess tumor rate above the spontaneous background rate in the experimental dosage range.
3. Connect a straight line from the origin to the point on the upper confidence limit at the lowest experimental dosage.
4. Obtain upper limits of risk for low dosages or, conversely, dosages corresponding to low upper limits of risk from the interpolation line obtained in Step 3.

Neither the linear extrapolation procedure adopted in the 1979 proposal nor the linear interpolation procedure adopted in this reproposal should be construed as a mechanistic model of carcinogenicity. FDA selected the linear interpolation procedure primarily because of all the procedures that do not disregard data from a chronic bioassay, the linear interpolation procedure is the least likely to underestimate risk.

The futility of attempting to select an extrapolation procedure based on how closely the procedure can describe the observed data and then predict risk at a low dose was illustrated in one of the comments. Six different models, each with a different biological rationale, were compared. The models were the one-hit, Weibull, logistic, log-probit, multi-hit, and multi-stage. The data used were derived from the ED_{01} study conducted at FDA's National Center for Toxicological Research. Because this study was specifically designed to investigate the carcinogenic response in the low dose region, many of the deficiencies found in studies designed to give only qualitative answers about carcinogenicity were not present. For liver neoplasms, the Weibull, logistic, and log-probit models could equally describe responses in the observed regions, but the predicted responses at a dose of 10 parts per billion varied by a factor of 10^{12}. For bladder hyperplasia, none of the models even came close to describing the observed responses.

APPENDIX 5

Physical and Radiological Characteristics of Radon and Radon Daughters

Table A5.1. Physical Characteristics of Radon and Its Daughters

Isotope	Atomic Number	Melting Point (°C)	Boiling Point (°C)	Density (g/mℓ)
Radon	86	−71	−62	9.73
Polonium	84	252	971	9.4
Lead	82	327.4	1750	11.34
Bismuth	83	271	1420	9.8

Table A5.2. Half-Lives and Energies of Radioisotopes in U-238 Decay Series

Isotope	Half-Life[a]	α-Energies (MeV)	β-Energies (MeV)	γ-Energies (MeV)	Internal Conversion
Radon-222	3.825 d	5.48 – 100%	—	—	—
Polonium-218	3.05 m	6.00 – 100%	? – 0.02%	—	—
Astatine-218	1.3 s	6.70 – 0.02% 6.65 – 0.001%	? – very weak		
Radon-218	1.9×10^{-2} s	7.13 – very weak	—	0.61 — very weak	—
Lead-214	26.8 m	—	0.59 – 56% 0.65 – 44%	0.24 0.30 0.35 others—weak	—
Bismuth-214	19.9 m	5.5 – 0.04%	0.4 – 9% 1.0 – 23% 1.51 – 40% 1.88 – 9% 3.26 – 19%	0.61 most 1.12 abundant 1.76 14 others to 2.43 MeV	—
Polonium-214	1.6×10^{-4} s	7.68 – 100%	—	several—very weak	—
Thallium-210	1.3 m	—	1.96 – 0.04%		—
Lead-210	22 y	—	0.017 – 85% 0.063 – 15%	0.047 – 5%	80%
Bismuth-210	5.01 d	$5.06 - 1.7 \times 10^{-4}$%	1.17 – 100%	—	—
Polonium-210	138.4 d	5.305 – 100%	—	$0.8 - 1.2 \times 10^{-3}$%	—
Thallium-206	4.2 m	—	$1.51 - 1.17 \times 10^{-4}$%	—	—
Lead-206	Stable	—	—	—	—

[a] d = day; h = hour; m = minute; s = second; y = year; IC = internal conversion; MeV = million electron volts (Wilson, 1966).

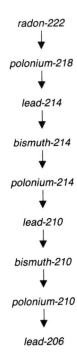

radon-222

↓

polonium-218

↓

lead-214

↓

bismuth-214

↓

polonium-214

↓

lead-210

↓

bismuth-210

↓

polonium-210

↓

lead-206

Figure A5.1.   Radon-222 decay scheme. Major decay products (greater than 0.02%
occurrence) are shown.

APPENDIX 6

Definitions of Radiological Terms

curie (Ci):

3.7×10^{10} disintegrations/second, 3.7×10^{10} becquerels

picocurie (pCi):

10^{-12} curies, 0.037 becquerels. 1 pCi per liter of air (pCi/ℓ) equals 37 becquerels per cubic meter

rem:

1 joule/kg, 0.01 seivert

working level (WL):

1.3×10^5 MeV/liter of air of potential alpha energy from polonium-218, lead-214, bismuth-214 and polonium-214 combined. Also defined as 100 picocuries per liter of air of radon-222 at equilibrium with polonium-218, lead-214, bismuth-214 and polonium-214.

alternate definition: 0.00103 (polonium-218) + 0.00507 (lead-214) + 0.00373 (bismuth-214) + 6×10^{-10} (polonium-214). Parentheses indicate activity concentration in pCi/ℓ.

189

working level month (WLM): 1 working level × 170 hours of exposure or any combination of working levels and time which are equivalent (e.g., 0.5 working levels × 340 hours, 85 working levels × 2 hours).

APPENDIX 7

Calculation of Working Level Months

Working level months (WLM) is a measure of the potential alpha energy of radon's short-lived daughters through polonium-214 (see definition in Appendix 6). The calculation of WLM requires assumptions regarding the equilibrium among the short-lived daughters and between the daughters and radon.

The equilibrium among the daughters is usually expressed as the ratio of activity concentrations:

polonium-218/lead-214/bismuth-214 and polonium-214

Due to the very short half-life of polonium-214 (1.6×10^{-4} seconds), the activity concentrations of bismuth-214 and its daughter polonium-214 are essentially the same. Consequently, they are usually expressed by a single value in the ratio. In the risk assessment example given in Chapter 8, the ratio used was 1/0.6/0.4. This ratio is typical of those found in homes (Hofmann, 1980). The ratio has also been hypothesized for mining environments (Berteig, 1981). Consequently, the radon daughter ratio used in the risk assessment is appropriate for both the environment of the experimental group and the risk group. Few actual measurements of daughter activity concentrations have been made.

The ratio between the short-lived daughters and radon is referred to as the equilibrium factor, or F. The equilibrium factor is defined as follows (UNSCEAR, 1977; Johassen, 1981; Kasuda, 1980):

$$F = \frac{0.103 \ (Po-218) + 0.507(Pb-214) + 0.373(Bi-214) + 6 \times 10^{-8}(Po-214)}{(Rn-222)}$$

OR

$$= 100 \frac{WL}{(Rn-222)}$$

Parentheses indicate activity concentrations in pCi/ℓ.

The equilibrium factor is related to the ventilation rate and other characteristics such as pressure and humidity. Higher ventilation rates generally produce lower F values and lower radon daughter concentrations. One air change per hour results in an F value of approximately 0.5 (UNSCEAR, 1982). In the example in Chapter 8, the equilibrium factor used was 0.5. This value was selected because it is the value determined by the United Nations Scientific Committee on the Effects of Ionizing Radiation (UNSCEAR) as the average indoor value worldwide (UNSCEAR, 1982). It may be somewhat lower than the values found in mining environments. The Swedish study used in this risk assessment estimated an F value of 0.7. Values were not given for the Czechoslovakian or Colorado studies. However, the values have been estimated to be 0.7 in the preventilation period in mines and 0.3 in the postventilation period. Since these two studies cover a time period when ventilation changes were beginning to be made, a value of 0.5 is appropriate. The differences in WLM which result from minor differences in F values (e.g., 0.5 versus 0.7) are not very significant at average or low exposures (e.g., 9 WLM).

For a more detailed explanation of radon daughter ratios and F values, see the UNSCEAR Reports of 1977 and 1982 (UNSCEAR, 1977, 1982). The activity concentrations of radon and its daughters used in this risk assessment are shown in Table A 7.1, along with the corresponding working levels and lifetime cumulative working level months. The working level months listed in Table A 7.1 are based on 75 years of exposure and 90% indoor occupancy time. Using the working level of 0.0025 listed in Table A 7.1 and the definition of working level months given in Appendix 6, working level months were calculated as follows:

$$WLM = \frac{0.0025 \ WL \cdot 8760 \ hours/year \cdot 75 \ years \cdot 0.9 \ occupancy \ factor}{170} = 9$$

Table A 7.1.   Working Levels, Working Level Months, Radon and Radon Daughter Activity Concentrations

Working Levels	Lifetime Working Level Months[a]	Radon–222 (pCi/ℓ)	Polonium–218 (pCi/ℓ)	Lead–214 (pCi/ℓ)	Bismuth–214 (pCi/ℓ)	Polonium–214 (pCi/ℓ)
0.0025	9	0.5	0.45	0.27	0.18	0.18
0.025	87	5	4.5	2.7	1.8	1.8
0.25	870	50	45	27	18	18
0.50	1739	100	90	54	36	36

[a]Lifetime working level months are based on 75 years of exposure and 90% indoor occupancy time (591,300 hours).

INDEX